# Rock Your Business

## How to Stand Out, Attract High Caliber Clients, and Create a Rush of New Sales

## Kristin Thompson
## and 9 Rock Star Entrepreneurs

Prominence Publishing

**PROMINENCE**
PUBLISHING

Rock Your Business Copyright © 2020 by Kristin Thompson

Published by Prominence Publishing
www.Prominencepublishing.com


ISBN: 978-1-988925-62-2

# Table of Contents

# Introduction

*"Life is short. Let's rock your business"*

The inspiration for this book stemmed from my desire to bring together great entrepreneurs who the world deserves to know.

And one of those entrepreneurs is YOU.

My colleagues and I collaborated with the hope to help you gain more visibility, attract more business, and stay happy & healthy along the way too! Because when you thrive, and when you rise up, you take other people with you. Your success impacts your family, your friends, your clients, and the people who work for you too!

The strategies inside this book cover an array of ideas to help you get known, develop your client attract strategies, and feel amazing while you're growing your business.

Business doesn't have to be about constantly pushing, endless nights spent away from family and loved ones, and eventually burning out.

You can rock your business by using the strategies that resonate with YOU, the ones you know you can maximize, as you consider your strengths... and what works for your lifestyle.

So, even though this book is full of actionable tips, you might not use every chapter of this book, and that's okay.

The most important thing is that you take action on at least ONE great tip. One good idea implemented well, can change everything. Isn't that exciting?

So enjoy the journey, find the strategies that speak to you, and have a blast rocking your business to the next level!

And don't ever forget.... YOU ROCK!

Kristin Thompson

# Rock Your Business with Speaking

By Kristin Thompson

Imagine for a moment that you're speaking to a group of 100 ideal clients. They're taking notes, laughing at your jokes, hanging onto your words! They are lit up by your ideas. And, best of all, at the end of your talk you invite them to work with you... and they all come running toward you with order forms in hand! Now you have a rush of new visibility, leads, and instantly happy paying clients in the room.

This is the joy of rockin' your talk online or off to grow your business.

Even better? You don't need to be a professional keynote speaker to enjoy results like this. You really need to be a teacher at heart. And I bet you are!

So, I want to share with you how creating one rockin' talk could very well solve every challenge your business could ever face... even if you don't see yourself as a "public speaker."

And, if you're already used to leading meetings or presentations, this will get you excited to take your speaking and your business to the next level.

Whether you're a coach, consultant, author, or expert, you can become more visible and more leveraged by delivering one well-crafted talk that turns an audience of strangers into a rush of new leads, clients, and cash for your business. This is exactly how I grew my business, and now I want to share my secrets with you.

Your talk will not just help you make more money, it will also help you serve the world in a bigger, brighter way. Here is my promise to you:

I promise that if you read on with an open mind, you will understand three keys that will change your business forever and help you get started speaking to serve more people and grow your business. So, you can join me in rockin' your talk online and off!

## Are you carrying buckets or are you building a pipeline?

If you're marketing products and services one-by-one, selling people one-by-one, and delivering your products and services one-by-one, it's very limiting. It's kind of like carrying a bucket of water back forth every time you need water for your family. It gets the job done, sure, but it's not the most efficient or scalable way of doing things. It's hard to gain momentum and you'll get maxed out quickly.

But if we build you a pipeline, that would change the game all together!

Think of it this way. The **pipe** is your talk. It's the thing that draws people in to your business. The **spigot** is the moment you make an offer for the audience to come to buy your product or service. This is how you can transform a lead into a client. And the **container** the water would flow into? Well, that is the product or service into which you put your customers.

If you use your talk to market and sell your products and services, you get to share your message once to many ideal clients all at the same time! So, even if we changed nothing else in your business, we've already given you a way to create massive leverage and momentum.

As a bonus, if we can make the product or service you deliver more leveraged, too (like an online course, a workshop, group coaching, or consulting of some kind), then we can keep selling without a limit on delivery!

The goal is NOT to create lots of talks. The goal is to create one ROCKIN' talk, and deliver it over again to fresh audiences (online and off) who will be excited to learn about you and your business.

In my Rock Your Talk program, I take you through 5 keys in a 5-week series... but, to keep this simple, I want to share with you the three biggest keys to success to help you get started.

The first key is to create your own rock star positioning.

The second key is to create your highly converting talk—one that serves and sells.

And how you can easily monetize your message!

Sound good? Okay Let's dive in a little further!

First let's address a few common MINDSET ROADBLOCKS.

These are the things that might be standing in your way (or at least slowing you) from really being able to get out there and make a big impact with your message by getting in front of audiences.

## CONCERN #1: "Don't be a show off"

If you're like me, you were raised to be humble. And that's a great thing. However, feeling like you "shouldn't be a show-off" can also hold you back, from feeling free to lead the room and be yourself. The truth is... Every room needs a leader, and when you're at the front the room, that leader is YOU. It's your job to manage the experience that the audience has, so don't shy away.

Someone out there is waiting to hear the message through you.

It's not about you being a show-off, because your talk actually isn't about you. Your talk is about reaching and helping that one person who needs your message so badly right now. So be brave, and remember that people would rather be entertained and led by you when you're at the front of the room.

I'll say it again because it's super important: You can be bold and confident because tour talk is not about you, but about serving your audience with your area of expertise.

## CONCERN #2: "I'm not a speaker"

You might be thinking, "I wasn't born a speaker." or "I haven't given any talks yet." These are not reasons to get started and I'll tell you why.

I definitely didn't come out of the womb with a microphone in hand, tap-dancing across stages, and odds are neither did you. In fact, I'm a pretty nervous speaker, if you can believe it.

The good news is that like most everything in life, speaking is a learned skill.

And the great news is that in this chapter, and even more so in our Rock Your Talk Program, I share some high impact, simple strategies you can start learning today that will kickstart your results.

## "Authority takes a lot of time."

It is a total mistake to believe that all of this has to be slow and plodding. Is there some work involved in any worthwhile endeavor? Of course. But we're going to talk about how you can fast-track it!

You'll get to benefit from my years of experience and remove some of the mistakes I made in the beginning, so that results come faster.

When you learn how to take advantage of high-visibility speaking gigs online and off, done properly you will gain instant authority and credibility.

You can take a quantum leap forward, just by learning simple speaking strategies (and I'll share some with you in this guide and in the speaking webinar, too).

## YOUR OPPORTUNITIES ARE LIMITLESS

There are lots of opportunities right now – more than ever before. It's become easier for your message and your business to be seen and heard, in person and online, too!

- Speaking at Events, Meetings, and Conferences
- Online Classes and Webinars
- YouTube Videos
- Radio and TV Interviews
- Podcast Interviews
- Live Streams
- Live Events (online or in person)
- Workshops (online or in person)
- Masterminds (online or in person)
- Retreats (online or in person)

These are all opportunities for you to be seen and heard — and opportunities to grow your business, too.

All of that is great, but if you are attracted to me, it's probably because you also know that I'm really about serving.

It's in the very name of our business.... Speak. Serve. Grow.

I like making lots of money; I like showing you how to make lots of money. And I like doing that with integrity and in a spirit of service.

The revenue boost is great, but when you're really making a difference in someone's life, those are the moments that will last a lifetime.

For me, helping people and seeing them thrive because of something I shared with them... well, that's the thing that wakes me in the morning, and helps me push through the hard days; and it will for you too.

## PROVEN & ROAD-TESTED STRATEGIES

By the way, I suppose I should let you know that I know what I'm talking about. I've personally invested well over $150,000 in my own training and mentorship.

And I've given hundreds of talks online and off, to small groups around a board room table to big audiences on stages with bright lights.

I road-tested speaking and selling for my own business for years – not months, not weeks, but for years, with consistent results – before I ever turned around and started sharing with anybody else.

And now I've had the great blessing of being able to help thousands of business owners learn how to rock their talk and grow their business.

- Chelsey Marie came to me when she was just 20 years old, and was quickly generating $15,000 months!

- Mary B had a life coach business when we transformed her business, her brands, and her talk, leading to her first $70,000.00 month.

- My client Cat just gave her FIRST talk ever, generating $10,100 with just 16 people in the room.

- Sherri-Lee has been leading online workshops and has generated as much in the first 6 months of this year, as she did all last year.

The list goes on and on, and I share this with you not to brag, but to reassure you that this works, for those of you who put it into action! Let's get into it!

First, you want to get yourself highly visible in the marketplace in a way that's going to benefit your business because you're going to know how to capitalize on that moment by rocking your talk. We're going to do that in a way that will grow your revenue and your business.

Speaking helped me take my own business from generating $30,000 a year to generating $30,000.00 months, and even $300,000.00 on weekends. It still blows my mind to this day! And one thing people always say is... wow love that talk title! Love your look! Love your brand!

Your brand is what will help you POP even in a crowded room or industry.

## KEY #1: YOUR BRAND PERSONALITY ARCHETYPE

What is visibility and branding and standing out really about?

Jeff Bezos famously said, "Branding is about what people say when you leave the room."

The worst thing that people could say about you when you leave the room is nothing. And, unfortunately for most people out there, that's what's happening.

You go to a networking group, you mingle, people enjoy meeting you, but they don't really get what you do ... and then you leave. Honestly, the worst thing that can happen is that your business is forgettable.

It's not easy to stand out. In fact, let's play a game of "Where's Waldo?" This is a stock photo with me added in on the right, and sadly I blend right in! (you can go ahead and laugh).

To stand out, you don't need to be crazy. You don't need to have purple stripes in your hair. What stands out the most in today's world is YOU being 100% authentically you.

In the picture below you can Ali Brown on the left. She is as beautiful as a Barbie doll and smart as a whip, very glamorous. Kendall Summerhawk is in the picture on my right. She is smart, sharp, and very earthy. She lives on a ranch in Arizona, and wears cowgirl boots and that's her vibe.

There I am in the middle. I'm the "Rock Your Talk" girl. And that's what's I'm known for... bring the fun and hot content, too! We're all being 100% true to who we are and we are all successful. So, it's important to remember there is not one way to be in order to be successful.

The most important thing to be is 100% YOU.

## YOUR BRAND PERSONALITY BLUEPRINT

One of the ways I help clients stand out is by uncovering their Unique Brand Personality.

Archetype. It is step one of my course, Rock Your Talk, and it's the first thing I do with coaching clients, too. It's a critical step that will infuse everything else that we're going to do together, from creating your product to the way you look to what your website looks like. It is infused into everything.

I created the Rock Your Talk "Brand Personality Blueprint" to help my clients stand out while staying in alignment with your true personality and authentic style.

## HOW TO UNCOVER YOUR ARCHETYPE

First, look at the center of the Brand Personality Blueprint. Which of the four core drivers means the MOST to you in your business: Are you driven to create a sense of Belonging, Stability, Freedom, or Change?

Which one of these core drivers do you VALUE over the others?

Then, based on the core driver you value most, you'll see it narrows the 12 Personality Archetypes to three, and from there you can find your ONE main archetype.

By the way … We all have bits of ALL these personalities inside of us. So, I am not saying you are ONLY one thing. We're saying you have all of this inside of you — but which one is your leading trait in business, which serves your client, too.

Make sense?

In my business, I lead with the Rebel, I LOVE to create change. And while I value the other core drivers, also, change is something I will not surrender. I have Everywoman in my brand, I'm very approachable. I have a little bit of joker in me too! I'm very caring towards my clients, of course.

But what I lead with is Rebel, because above all else, I am about standing up for business owners and helping them be 100% authentic as they grow their businesses and their finances.

Uncover your core brand archetype (or two), and begin to use it to stand out in your market.

Your brand personality archetype influences:

- Your style when you're speaking and presenting
- Program and product titles
- Color choices
- Font choices
- Pictures
- Social media posts
- and more!

In other words, you're not going to see flowers and pastel colors and lots of uber-feminine cursive fonts on my website. It doesn't make sense with who I am. But, for somebody else, it does. So, you really want to align everything with your true personality. It will help you STAND OUT without mimicking market leaders.

This is key number one to your success.

## ACTION STEP:

Notice where you are showing your true, original personality and where it might be missing. Plus, you can download the Brand Personality Guide with templates and a video training at:

SpeakingReallyWorks.com

## KEY #2: Craft Your Rockin' Talk to Serve and Sell

Nothing beats the feeling of inspiring people to take action and grow in their life or business or body or health, or whatever it is you do... and that only happens if you close the room.

Let that sink in.

The best way to serve people is to work with them and give them a full transformation. In order to work with them, you need to invite them to work with you! Before I share some tips to help you rock your talk, you'll want to consider where do you want to be seen.

There are lots of opportunities for you to give talks and become visible.

There are more than 100,000 associations just in the United States alone. And, there are about as many associations in Canada, and then we have the remainder of the big, wide world.

Every association has local meetings that are usually every month, regional meetings, national meetings, meetings galore! And this is great news for you. Lots of opportunities to speak!

In the United States there are 1.8 million events, conferences, and trade shows. Just think of the thousands of people who are attending every year.

And right now, just as many events and workshops are happening online, and they are actually outperforming in person events.

There are about 550,000 podcasts right now, and many are GREAT opportunities for you to heard by ideal clients!

You can be a guest on someone's podcast and generate tons of visibility, leads, and even clients.

To help you be certain you take advantage of all these opportunities, here are the four things that you always want to make sure that you have or that you leave with when you give a talk. Get it locked in.

By the time you leave, your talk should give you more: Credibility, Leads, Clients, and Cash. Leaving with compliments is not enough. We want every talk to help you thrive and grow!

The first batch of clients you get from a speaking gig should be right there in the room... with no follow-up, no strategy sessions. You give your talk, make your offer, and you leave with order forms in hand. BOOM! It's the best feeling in the world!

And then you can get a second wave of clients by following up with people after your talk, too.

I WAS ABOUT TO BAIL ON MY FIRST TALK

Eight is the number of people I spoke to at my very first talk. Eight people! Seriously, I should be embarrassed. Not even 18. I can count then on two hands.

Ninety-nine is the number of times I was going to leave because I was so scared (remember this is a talk to just eight people). Yet I was about to walk away without even giving it because, as I said early, I'm not a "natural speaker.

This is not a story to be cute or dramatic. I sat in the parking lot in front of the building. I got there an hour early and I was drinking a Starbucks, and I was thinking...

"Forget these people. I'm going home!"

I'm being totally honest. Embarrassing but true. Even though it was a small group, and they were super nice, and, let's face it, there aren't any dire consequences if it doesn't go well... I was still terrified.

I thought, "This is nuts. I don't know why I agreed to do this. I'm probably going to throw up on these people. I should just go home and pretend it never happened."

The thing that made me go up there was that my Mom and Dad raised me right. They raised me to be a good person. So, I mustered up whatever courage I could and went upstairs to give the talk so that I wouldn't leave this group high and dry.

This is how big of a chicken I am by the way. So, if I can do it... so can YOU.

Miraculously, I sold three tickets to a workshop. (I'll tell you why that is in a moment — and its good news for you!)

Three tickets at $400 each sold in a room of eight people... not too shabby for a girl just getting started. The talk generated $1,200.00 in sales. Remember, there were only 8 people in the room and I barely knew what I was doing. So, I was starting to get pretty darn excited.

Twelve hundred dollars might not be a lot of money to you right now, and I certainly make much more from my talks now. But, for an hour's work, I thought it was pretty cool. That day I unlocked the magic of speaking and selling and I wasn't going to stop there.

And the reason WHY I was able to generate sales, even though I wasn't at my best, was because the talk I gave was crafted properly. Remember this! Your talk needs to be crafted properly for it to work. I'll show you talk structure in a moment.

Of course, I have gone on to give talks that generate $25,000.00, $50,000.00, and more. I did a webinar from my home office just the other day to a few people that generated $20,000.00 in new sales of our entry-level program.

There is so much you can do once you get started. It doesn't matter where you are now... all that matters is that you begin to see how speaking can lift your business up into the next level for you.

Now I could write a whole book just about crafting your talk. For today, I thought I'd share with you the high-level overview of the talk structure. You can use this as a guide for a talk, sales presentation, or Facebook live stream!

In the Rock Your Talk program we go into deeper detail in each section, like HOW you introduce yourself, or tell your story, and how to teach your main points. But for now, I think this is a good start.

In the Rock Your Talk program, we go into deeper detail in each section, like HOW you introduce yourself, or tell your story, and how to teach your main points. But for now, I think this is a good start. You can download this structure and a training on each part of it at www.SpeakingReallyWorks.com.

The main thing I want to point out here is that the beginning of your talk is all about starting strong, gaining the audience's interest, and getting it interacting with you! The middle is all about adding value with your main points (the teaching points) and making sure the points get some BIG AH-HAs so that the audience is interested in diving in and learning more! Your offer is about inviting those people, who are loving the topic, not to leave their interest in the room, but rather step up and work with you in a deeper way!

# HOW GOOD PEOPLE ACCIDENTALLY
# GIVE BAD TALKS

Good people do give bad talks. Or, even worse, sometime people give really good talks that don't convert. But there's always a good reason why, and it can happen to the best of us. Here are a few common challenges that might be holding you back or slowing your results.

## Changing topics

If you are always out speaking on different topics, and your message is all over the map, it will slow your results and really sabotage your growth. Doesn't matter if you're on a podcast, or a stage, or a Facebook live, your topic needs to stay focused, and your message stay consistent.

## One way to profit

In the beginning, this is what I did. I had a workshop. One workshop. That was the only thing I offered. There was no next step, there was no higher level, there was just one thing. (Not a good idea.) So, working with me was a yes/no decision.

Ideally you want to have the right offer for the right person. I suggest for most coaches, authors, and consultants an entry-level product or service (something under $1K), a mid-level $3k-10k, and high-level product or service ($10K-$100k).

This way people can progress and continue graduating to higher levels! And, you have an entry level offer that's perfect for selling at the end of your talk!

## Lecture

If your talk isn't crafted properly, if you don't know how to deliver it naturally, you could accidentally end up talking "at" people. Lectures are notoriously boring. So, we want to avoid lecturing people. We want to avoid being boring.

Keep your talks interesting and interactive. Imagine your talk is more like a mini workshop! You can have people take notes, raise their hands, respond to questions, and shout things out. This way it's fun and interactive, because an audience that will play with you, will buy from you!

## Hard sell

No one likes a "hard sell," And I'm going to guess that you are not hard selling because very rarely are people attracted to me and my work who do that.

But what does happen is the fear of hard selling holds you back. In fact, you might be so afraid of hard selling that you're not making offers at all. You're just skipping the whole hoo-ha! That's very common and we'll talk about what to do instead in a moment.

I want to encourage you to shift your thinking here and consider your offer as a way to help those people who need you the most by inviting them to take the next step!

### The Command Any Room Commandment

Please join me and my clients in following the Command Any Room Commandment. Thou shall always have an offer. Thou shall deliver it with a spirit of service. Some of the time? No. Most of the time? No. Always have an offer.

In fact, I'm going to encourage you to have two offers:

A free offer and a paid offer.

I'll show you how this works, and why it's so brilliant in a moment. First you need an order form. An order form is a simple way for people to say yes right there in the room. You have to give people a way to say yes right then and there in your talk. So have an order form. It can be an 8x10 piece of paper that you print on your printer at home. It doesn't need to be complicated, but there are two things you want to include.

The very first box that people can check is for a free gift, and the next one is for a program that they can purchase – your entry level signature system.

Always have these two things. Why? The Free Gift is someone digital like a check list or a pdf or a video that will help people and it also allows you to stay in touch and follow up!

### The Paid Program

The paid program allows you actually to work with people and serve them in a bigger way. There are lots of different offers. For those of you who I get to work with in a bigger way, we can help you with that if you don't know what to offer.

The reality is that if you have information in your head, you have something to offer people at the end of your talk!

## HOW TO MONETIZE YOUR TALK

So, we've talked about how to stand out, how to craft your talk, and how important it is to monetize your message and make offers! I want to leave you with some ideas of what you can offer at the end of your talk.

Here are some ways you can monetize your message:

- **A Live Weekly Class or Training Series:** Choose your main topic and teach one step of your system each week for 5-6 weeks.

- **A Live Workshop:** Teach all the steps of your signature system in a workshop that is held in person or online.

- **A Home Study Program:** Record a series of classes that people can watch or listen to on their own, whenever they want. Consider offering 5-7-hour long modules max.

- **A Consultation:** Consultations are great if you offer a higher ticket program or service, or if you can't sell at the end of a speaking gig. They are also a good idea if you are good at handling one-on-one sales conversations. If you work with corporate clients, consultations are a great way to go.

**HOT TIP**: Don't call it a "Free Consultation." Give it a Rockin' Title, a Value, and a Limited number available.

Would you rather have a "free session" or a "Weight Loss Breakthrough Session worth $500.00"?

These one-on-one sales conversations are a great way to connect with and to convert people into higher end services or programs.

So now I'd like you to imagine you're speaking to 100 people. At the end of your talk, you make an offer for people to join your course, or attend your workshop. Let's say 20% of them say yes (that's a good but not record-breaking amount).

You now have 20 new clients in hand. If you offered your workshop at $597 a ticket, you've generated $11,940. If you change $1K for your program or workshop you've obviously generated $20,000.00.

Then remember once you're delivering your product or service you can invite up to the next level program.

Give your talk >>> Make Your Offer >>>Deliver Your Offer >>> Upsell into a High -end Offer

So, there's not ONE way to generate income from your talk, there are MANY.

You can profit from instant in-the-room sales after your talk.

You can profit from following up with people who did not buy in the room.

You can profit from people who bought your offer, and later up-level into a higher-level product, program, or service.

You can profit by getting referrals to additional places to speak and repeating your talk and your sales!

CHA CHING! Are you starting to see how powerful this is for your business?

## TIME TO TAKE ACTION and RISE UP

It's time to stop playing small. It's time to Rise Up.

Surround yourself with people walking the path you want to walk– people earning what you want to learn and playing at the level you want to play at that so you can create that new normal.

Don't hope and pray it works out. Decide. Decide to get up in front of rooms big and small.

Share your message, and do it in a way where you're always making an offer so that you can serve people in a bigger way and grow your business at the same time.

Your message is powerful, but it needs you to give it life. And somewhere out there is someone waiting to hear the message through you!

# About the Author

Kristin Thompson is a wife, a mother, and a mentor to rock star experts just like you. She calls herself an unlikely speaker, only resorting to speaking to help her business generate income during the economic downturn of 2009.

On her journey she developed her own system for speaking to groups with a spirit of service that also generated big waves of business.

Ten years ago, she made waves launching her Command Any Room program taking her business from $30,000 year to $175,000 working 3 days a week.

Seven years ago, she launched her first live event for speakers generating multiple-six-figures in a weekend.

Four years ago, she launched her Rock Your Talk course generating over $200,000 in sales in just 1 month.

And now, she's here to help you turn one talk into the engine that drives your visibility and your revenue to new levels.

Ready to get started? Visit www.SpeakingReallyWorks.com to gain instant access to the blueprint to use speaking to scale up more leads & sales in your business. and visit www.SpeakServeGrow.com anytime to connect with Kristin.

# Has Marketing Acquired A Bad Rap?

By Jennifer Covington

While you may have been turned off of marketing due to a negative experience in the past, please know, as a purpose-driven, soul-centered entrepreneur, you're perfectly primed to be great at marketing and do it in a really aligned way.

One issue my clients have when they first come to me is the lack of knowing how to market themselves authentically. You see, during the onset of online marketing, the space was dominated by spammy, often misleading, messages. The idea was to get people to purchase, get them in the door, and the commitment to deliver wasn't always there.

Maybe you have taken a course, or have received advice on how to use bait-and-switch methods to hook your client. Maybe you're familiar with the smoke-and-mirror strategies that old-school marketers put in place or you may be aware of some modern-day tactics that incorporate hard selling and shaming people into working with you.

## Your Strong Moral Compass

The issue is that if you're anything like me or my clients, you're unwilling to play games with people's trust and emotions. Even though you're dedicated to your work, you'd rather starve than dupe people into working with you.

So, what's a purpose-led, mission-driven, soul-centered entrepreneur to do?

Don't you worry, I'm just like you and I've got a simple formula you can follow to ensure you're regularly calling in your ideal clients while showing up fully as yourself in a really aligned and authentic way.

## You're in Luck!

First, here's the good news. You're in luck because being heart-led and soul-centered is what people are craving right now. The market, your audience, wants to see present, transparent, authentic people in their feeds, on their timelines, on TV, and in person. We all want to witness it when we're reading your words or hearing your voice, and the good news is that highlights your natural strengths and who you are!

Gone are the days of the infallible expert, or the flawless guru on the mountain top. All of that equals totally un-relatable in this modern day and age of marketing.

## The Secret to Your Success

That means all you need to do is uncover the best way for you to show up fully as you, in a genuine way, and your right clients are going to find you irresistible.

If you're not sure how to do that, worry not, I've got you covered!

# Marketing 101

Now, before we dive into the perfect solution for you, we need to break down exactly what *Marketing* is, in its most simple terms.

First, don't be intimidated by the word "marketing", since it's something you're likely doing naturally anyway.

Sometimes, to soften the word, I call it *Outreach* or I describe it as a way to *Shine Your Light*. Essentially, marketing is the manner in which you let an audience know who you are, what you do, and how you can help them solve a problem they may be experiencing in their life.

# Marketing to Consider

After working in the marketing departments of Fortune 500 companies for years and being trained by some of the best in the industry, I've learned the power of studying your market and knowing your marketing inside and out as the best way to attract those who make up your target market.

Let's define some of those terms so it all makes sense.

When referencing *Your Market*, we're really saying anyone in the general public who has the potential to buy your goods, services, or offers.

Now, Your Market breaks down into a few segments that you need to know: Your Cold Market, Your Warm Market, and Your Target Market

## Your Cold Market

Your cold market is comprised of people who don't yet know of you, they don't know what you do, and they don't yet know they need your goods and services.

## Your Warm Market

This is the population of people who are familiar with you and what you offer.

Note: The reason you podcast, tweet, email, post, etc., is to convert *Your Cold Market* into *Your Warm Market* – that is the root reason you partake in any *Marketing* activities at all!

Which brings us to the most important market of all, and that's *Your Target Market.*

## Your Target Market

*Your Target Market* is made up of the group of people who are actually excited about what you do, they know who you are, and they believe that what you do is the perfect solution to an issue that they may have.

The reason it's important to know the identity of *Your Target Market* is so you can spend all of your marketing efforts focused on them and no one else. When you're unclear as to who *Your Target Market* is, that's when you'll find yourself struggling to get conversions and make sales.

## You're Getting Warmer

In review, Marketing is simply the outreach you do to turn Your Cold Market into A Warm Market so that those who are in Your Target Market are able to experience you, learn from you, and eventually buy from you!

## YOUR ACTION PLAN:

When it comes to approaching your *Authentic Marketing Strategy*, you must take into account there are two distinct approaches you can take when connecting with your audience. Next, we're going to talk about exactly what those are.

When it comes to approaching your audience there are two paths you can choose.

1. Go Where They're Gathered
2. Attract Them Toward You

## Go Where They're Gathered

Part of your job as an effective marketer is to find out where your target market is hanging out. They may be physical hangouts or virtual hangouts (it's great if you can identify a mix of both), but the folks that make up your target market already gather somewhere. Do some research and find out where those places are!

## Attract Them Toward You

When you host your own workshop and invite your folks to your webinar happening next week, those are examples of you attracting your target market toward you. When you're attracting them, it's your responsibility to fill the seats or fill your calendar with the appointments. It's up to you to draw in your target market, based on what you know about them and their needs.

## Put It All Together

For best results, you'll want to mix these two paths together, remembering not to neglect in-person opportunities and virtual opportunities. You can see how customized your *Authentic Marketing Plan* can get and how the possibilities are seemingly endless!

Don't let that overwhelm you, there's a very specific way to approach which *Authentic Marketing Plan* is best for you, so next let's talk about *The 3 Pillars to Effective, Authentic, Soul-Centered Marketing* and exactly how to come up with your customized approach.

The Pillars to Effective, Authentic, Soul-Centered Marketing are:

- Consistency

- Authenticity

- Relatability

Any time you can nail those three pillars, your marketing efforts will feel connected, warm, and genuine. No need to worry about coming off like a sleazy, slimy spammer!

# Your 3-Step Checklist to Authentic Marketing Bliss!

Finally, here's the perfect checklist you can use truly to figure out where your *Marketing* efforts should go. It's simple, it's customized to you, and it's going to make you love *Marketing* once and for all!

## Ask Yourself These Three Simple Questions:

Where do I like to play?

Where are my ideal clients?

Where do I shine the brightest?

## Step 1:

First, consider where you like to play and where you like to show up, naturally. The #1 issue folks have with marketing themselves effectively is that they struggle with showing up *consistently*. However, by choosing a platform where you naturally play anyway, you're stacking the odds in your favor.

This can look like choosing the social media platform that you naturally gravitate toward, and it can also look like making the networking event you attend regularly part of your marketing plan.

You get to decide and this is the easiest step to get right. Just observe where you show up organically any given day and jot down some notes on what you observe, and then move on to Step #2.

## Step #2

Next you want to think about where your ideal clients hang out. This is an essential element to consider and you can't skip this step. There's no use in showing up somewhere consistently if the folks you're trying to attract aren't there to see you, witness you, and partake in your brilliance! So, the next thing you must take into account is where are your ideal clients are hanging out. Basically, you're now thinking about where they like to play.

You can learn this through asking your current clients, polling your newsletter list, or posting a survey on one of your social media channels. It's something you can ask in conversation at a networking event and you can even poll your peers and colleagues as long as they fit the profile of someone who would be an ideal client for you.

## Step #3

Finally, you'll want to consider where you shine the brightest. This one is my favorite things to talk about because it's the hidden gem of marketing yourself authentically. This may sound like step #1, but it's actually not!

Where you like to play and where you shine the brightest may not be the same places, and what I've found after working with a myriad of coaches, healers, & creative entrepreneurs in their businesses, **where we shine the brightest** tends to be the area we shy away from the most.

Maybe you're a great writer but you shy away from doing it because you judge yourself and think you're not great.

Maybe you're a dynamic speaker, but have stage fright so you never do it.

Maybe you're a natural at rapport building and you can work a room like a star, but you don't realize how magnetic you are.

THIS step tends to be the blind spot for most people, but THIS is where you unlock your magic and magnetism and where client attraction becomes a breeze.

I'll use myself as an example. I have the gift of the gab (translation: I talk a lot) and public speaking is an area where I shine the brightest.

The problem? I used to be *terrified* of speaking in public!

Maybe you've heard the statistic that most people on the planet fear public speaking more than they fear death. I absolutely fit in that category. There's a joke by Jerry Seinfeld, who observes that what that means is at any given funeral, the majority of the people would rather be in the casket than give the eulogy.

That was 100% ME!

However, at various times in my life, I would be "pushed onto stage," whether it was speaking at my grandma's 90th birthday, MCing for a non-profit event, or being called to talk about what I do for a living at various professional events.

Any time I spoke in front of a crowd, I would walk away with a new fan, a new business partner, a new client, or a new warm connection. What I found is that when I speak in public, I *convert* strangers into colleagues of some kind, quickly and easily – just by being myself.

What do I mean by convert?

The word *convert* or *conversion* simply means to turn one thing into something else. In marketing terms, it's when you've taken strangers and made them into someone interested in your work. They've opted in to know more, they've purchased something from you, they've leaned in somehow to let you know they're interested and officially part of your warm market (yay!).

### Here's How to Find Out Where YOU Shine the Brightest

Think about where people compliment you. Whether it's the prose on your website, your dynamic speaking ability, or your ability to connect deeply one-on-one, where do strangers, friends, or colleagues come up to you and say, "Oh my goodness, you're so good at that" or "You really touched me when I heard you speak/read your blog/had our one-on-one conversation." Pay attention to that feedback, there's gold there!

Ask some trusted colleagues, friends and even clients where appropriate. Since this is so close to you and likely a blind spot, you may need to enlist some outside help for you to SEE where you shine the brightest. You'll be amazed at how you'll get the same feedback over and over again. Once you ask 5-10 people where they think you show up the most powerfully and effectively, you'll absolutely walk away with your answer.

## A Note About This:

You may find that you get feedback that surprises you in an area where you may not feel that strong. Teresa came to me – not a strong writer – but everyone says even when she simply posts on social media or writes her blog, she gets a lot of feedback and people resonate with her deeply through her writing.

Or, the same in my story. I got the feedback that I shine brightly when I'm in person speaking, but I was terrible due to freaking out internally anytime I was "called to the stage."

In both of these cases, the answer to this issue is the same. It doesn't mean everyone is lying to you – **it's simply a case of needing to skill up.**

Once Teresa committed to doubling down on her writing, she took some writing courses and wrote every day, even if some days the writing wasn't her best. By getting into the practice of writing every day, she got faster and better at expressing herself through the written word.

Or, in my case, I hired and continue to hire speaking coaches and teachers to help me step on stage confidently and effectively to use a gift I already have and channel it into something positive and intentional.

So, it's okay to need to practice and really hone your gift, all the greats do it. Take the course, hire the coach, and practice, practice, practice. Serena Williams does it, Beyoncé does it, and now you will, too!

You DID IT!

Now you have the simple, yet effective, roadmap on how to market yourself authentically – now it's up to you to go out there, shine your light, and connect with your people!

# About the Author

Jennifer Covington is a Life Coach & Business Strategist and Queen Way-Maker for World-Changers. She works with coaches, healers and creative entrepreneurs who are looking to reach $10,000 dollars monthly doing work they enjoy that also positively impacts the world.

Jennifer has had the pleasure of working with talented mission-driven women (and some cool men) who are dedicated and committed not only to doing work that lights them up, but doing it in an integrous way.

Jennifer has had the pleasure of working with Fortune 500 giants such as Anheuser-Busch, MGM Studios, and 20th Century Fox. She spent 3 years in Ecuador teaching small business development to poverty-stricken single mothers and orphaned youth as a means of livelihood and sustainability.

From these experiences, Jennifer has learned what it takes (no matter who you are) to create, build, and run a freedom-based business from the ground up. Her genius lies in her ability to help you turn your passion into profit so you can make the positive impact you were destined to make in the world.

## A Gift For You:

www.jennifercovington.com/authenticmarketing

# 3 Steps to Authentic Leadership Excellence

By Susan J. Ryan

Our world needs great leaders! More than 10,000 individuals born between the years 1944 and 1964, who are commonly referred to as Baby Boomers[1], are retiring every day in the United States.[2] This is resulting in a shortage of excellent experienced leaders who are also mentors for emerging leaders, themselves who now need to grow into leadership excellence more quickly than ever before.

For more than thirty years, I have been guiding individuals, committed to unprecedented success in their lives and businesses, to become the leaders others follow. Clients raise their self-awareness of *who* they are and gain clarity about their uniquely greatest talents, skills, and abilities – their Prodigy Zone™. They connect with their purpose and create their authentic vision that evolves with them throughout their lives, continuously inspiring them and those they lead. They feel fulfilled and they feel great about themselves as they create their unique positive impact. We

---

[1] https://www.raconteur.net/hr/senior-management-gap-left-retiring-baby-boomers
[2] https://www.investopedia.com/articles/personal-finance/032216/are-we-baby-boomer-retirement-crisis.asp

work together with the product and service offerings of my company, *Sue Ryan Solutions*, through professional speaking, individual and group coaching, workshops, courses, and books.

- Have you ever felt something is missing? You know you're not doing exactly what you're meant to be doing. You aren't sure how to figure out what it is and wonder how it is you feel this way.

- Have you ever struggled to work successfully with team members? You don't see things the same way and know it shouldn't have to be so difficult.

- Have you ever stepped away from doing something you enjoyed because someone else influenced your view of your talents, skills, and abilities?

- Do you ever find it difficult to set goals and, even if you achieve them, don't feel satisfied?

Three Steps to Authentic Leadership Excellence introduces you to the answers to these questions so you:

- Know yourself in a meaningful way, including your personality style, how and why you view the world the way you do, and what drives your actions when times are good and when times are stressful.

- Discover your uniquely greatest talents, skills and abilities. Create the vision for your life that supports you continuously maximizing your potential while feeling great about yourself.

- Lead yourself with excellence from the inside out. Model this with others through clarity and confidence, collectively achieving the positive impact that continues to evolve as others grow into their leadership excellence.

Authentic leadership excellence is important in all the aspects of our lives. Focusing on the professional aspect:

- A 2018 Gallup Poll[3] identified organizations with strong leadership and employee engagement were at least 21% more profitable than those without.

- Gallup also identified that "Fewer than three in 10 employees strongly agree that their performance is managed in a way that motivates them to do outstanding work."[4]

- The 2019 Retention Report, researched by Work Institute,[5] found that 75% of the employees who quit could have been retained by employers, and that the replacement cost of an employee in the average salary range is $15,000 or more.

Imagine the positive impact authentic leadership excellence can have. Using the points above, if employees understood and felt connected with the vision of their leader, they would remain engaged and loyal. Turnover rates would be significantly reduced as employees applied their very best efforts to bring the vision to

---

[3] https://news.gallup.com/poll/241649/employee-engagement-rise.aspx

[4] https://www.gallup.com/workplace/245786/gallup-reports-share-leaders-2019.aspx

[5]https://info.workinstitute.com/hubfs/2019%20Retention%20Report/Work%20Institute%202019%20Retention%20Report%20final-1.pdf

life. These would lead to a reduction in expenses and an increase in profitability that would, most likely, far exceed the 21% that Gallup identified.

Authentic leadership excellence is the ultimate in equal opportunity and inclusiveness. Excellent leaders, such as UCLA Basketball coach John Wooden,[6] emerge over years of consistently leading from the clarity their purpose and values. Leaders such as 2018 Marjory Stoneman Douglas High School shooting survivor, Cameron Kasky,[7] emerge as the result of a defining moment. Leadership excellence is the result of our ability to influence and empower ourselves and others.

There are no restrictions to being an authentically excellent leader. There is no single path to becoming one. There is one place to start – *with us.*

## Step 1: Start with Who? – You!

How do you become your greatest leading others? Begin by becoming your greatest by leading yourself. How do you become your greatest leading yourself? Begin by knowing yourself through awakening your self-awareness. Why is self-awareness so important? This is your motivation, your catalyst, to discovering your true potential. You feel fulfilled and know how to define success and satisfaction in all aspects of your life. One example of the importance of self-awareness is found in the results of a

---

[6] https://www.thewoodeneffect.com/about-coach/
[7] https://www.bbc.com/news/stories-47217467

study focused on traits that predict executive success. Organizational consulting firm Green Peak Partners found that "A high self-awareness score was the strongest predictor of overall success."[8]

Unquenchable curiosity is the key to beginning your journey of self-awareness. There's a good reason young children ask questions all the time – they learn through curiosity! Our personalities are formed in early childhood. They are influenced by our genetics, family and community environments, and profound events.[9] Once formed, they become highly unconscious to us and we rarely go back to evaluate if they still serve us. Awaken your awareness of your thoughts, actions, emotions, and beliefs through revisiting the unquenchable curiosity of your youth:

- When you use a word to describe something, ask yourself if you clearly understand the definition for yourself or if you are using someone else's definition.

- Think about why you quit something you used to enjoy. Did you simply become disinterested? Did you quit because someone told you that you weren't any good or would never be any good? Would you like to try again?

- Are you aware of how you act and react when under stress?

- Are there areas in your life in which you would like to invest more time and energy? Why?

---

[8] https://greenpeakpartners.com/wp-content/uploads/2018/09/Green-Peak_Cornell-University-Study_What-predicts-success.pdf
[9] http://www.healthofchildren.com/P/Personality-Development.html

- Are there areas in your life in which you would like to invest less time and energy? Why?

Once you've raised your level of awareness, you're ready to discover valuable insights into your natural personality style, your way of looking at the world, how you process events, and how you relate with others. One valuable resource for accomplishing this is through a powerful personal assessment called the Enneagram.[10] The Enneagram provides a wide range of insights into your personality, making it a valuable resource for your growth for years to come. There are a wide variety of Enneagram assessments available, from free[11] to comprehensive.[12]

These insights serve as your catalyst to gain clarity on your uniquely greatest talents, skills, and abilities – your Prodigy Zone™.

## Step 2: Discover Your Prodigy Zone™

Each of us are prodigies, many of us are undiscovered. A prodigy is someone with extraordinary talents or abilities.[13] Each of us have them. We may have stopped in our exploration before we discovered our prodigy. We are meant to, we deserve to, be our greatest and live our best lives! This is living in our prodigy zone.

---

[10] https://www.merriam-webster.com/dictionary/enneagram
[11] https://www.techjunkie.com/best-free-enneagram-tests/
[12] https://ianmorgancron.com/assessment
[13] https://www.dictionary.com/browse/prodigy

An insightful way for you to begin is with a simple exercise that has you consider all aspects of your life. Create two lists:

- The first list is things you like, things that energize you, things you want to do.

- The second list is things you don't like, things that drain you of energy, things you don't want to do.

Throughout the activities of your life, become aware of what you like and don't like and simply record them on the appropriate list. For example, you like working on teams, you prefer working alone, you don't like confrontation, you like volunteering, you don't like fundraising. There is no scoring or prioritizing in this exercise. It doesn't matter if something is on the list multiple times.

As you continue to become aware of what you like and what you don't like, you'll also become aware of finer distinctions. For example, you may have said "I don't like to travel." You may realize there are parts of travel you like and parts you don't like. Begin adding the finer distinctions. This is also a powerful and valuable team exercise.

After recording items for a period of time, perhaps one month, look at what you've recorded on each list. The areas you like, that energize you, help you discover your prodigy zone. These are the areas for you to place your focus, invest time for continuous improvement, and participate in as much as possible. You become known for, and sought after in, these areas.

What about the things you don't like, that drain you of energy, that you don't want to do? These are the items that are not in your Prodigy Zone™. Here are several options to address them:

- First, see if you can find others who do like them. For example, on a team, you have great ideas. You don't like putting together all the details required to bring them to life. Find the team member who does like working with details. See if there is something they don't like to do, that you do, and swap. On teams, it helps members get to know each other while increasing engagement, performance and satisfaction.

- Second, see if you can gain a different perspective on what it is you don't like. Can you look at it through the lens of something you do like? For example, you don't like to cook but you feel great when you have more energy. Can you connect cooking as an important step to gaining more energy and choose to do it?

- Third, for those remaining items, own that you don't like to do them. Based on your personality style, determine when it's easiest for you to do things you don't like to do and continue trying to find someone who does like to do them.

When you clearly understand your natural personality style, the lens through which you view our world, how your emotions impact your choices, what's important to you, what energizes you, and what drains you of energy, you have access to your greatest potential and possibilities. You know *who* you are. You discover your authentic voice.

A valuable gift of this clarity is that you no longer live through self-doubts and limiting beliefs of the past. If they come up, you now have choices that move you toward excellence. Andy Stanley, Senior Pastor of North Point Ministry, explains: "Your past reminds you, but doesn't define you."[14] This clarity serves as your catalyst to create the vision of who you know you must become, what you know you are meant to do in our world, and how these become your authentic leadership excellence.

## Step 3: Lead Yourself

You've elevated your self-awareness, discovered and learned how to live in your prodigy zone, and have options for managing what isn't in it. Now it's time to feel great about leading yourself with clarity, confidence, competence, and consistency:

- Purpose and Values - Gain clarity on your purpose and values; these are your "Why," your foundation. These make it easy for you to create your boundaries. They become the guideposts and guardrails that help you maintain consistency in your words and actions. You build trust first, and most importantly, in yourself. You earn trust from those around you. Your purpose and values give you the courage to make wise decisions that reduce both distractions and detractions. This is crucial when temptations of the immediate have the potential to distract you from achieving your ultimate goals. Business

---

[14] http://www.thesermonnotes.com/let-your-past-inform-not-control-your-decisions/

magnate, investor, and philanthropist, Warren Buffet, says: "The difference between successful people and really successful people is that really successful people say no to almost everything."[15] When you have the confidence to say "no" to what isn't aligned with your purpose and values, you create space to say "yes" to what is.

- Vision - Create your vision from the clarity of who you know you must become, with the passion of knowing you can. You know you are making choices that move you toward your vision. Your vision is not just about you; it's about the positive impact created because of who you become. When you invite others into bringing your vision to reality, they know with clarity how vital they are to its success.

- Gifts and Gaps - One of the most valuable benefits of self-awareness is both recognizing and accepting your natural gifts and gaps. We all have both. When you gain clarity on your gaps and accept them as an important part of who you are, you are able to share them with confidence and surround yourself with people who are strong in these areas. Collectively, you support each other in excellence that is greater than any one person can create.

- Practice mindset - We are rarely perfect at something in the beginning. When we do something and it isn't perfect, unfortunately, we often believe, or have been told,

---

[15] https://www.inc.com/marcel-schwantes/warren-buffett-says-this-is-1-simple-habit-that-separates-successful-people-from-everyone-else.html

we have failed. It is rather that the outcome is not what we anticipated; we are being given a meaningful opportunity to learn. Embrace these with the vulnerability of potential, not perfection. Over time you develop competence – your ability to do something successfully.[16] When you lead others who are learning, this mindset gives you the courage to share your emotions as you share your lessons. Instead of trying to impress others with your knowledge, you empower them to explore their potential and possibilities. When you model excellence, you inspire excellence.

- Permission - Give yourself permission to be your greatest version of yourself. When I was growing up, I observed others who were "more or better than" I was. I felt I was not good enough, I held myself to a standard that was theirs, not mine. Even when I achieved top performance, I wasn't satisfied. What I didn't realize at the time was that by holding myself to my perceived standard based on someone else, I couldn't become my best version of myself. Now that I have discovered this, I am committed to empowering as many people as possible to live their lives from this awesome, authentic place of satisfaction and sense of purpose. Give yourself permission to become your authentically greatest. You now know you can't settle for anything less.

---

[16] https://www.lexico.com/en/definition/competence

Authentically leading yourself with excellence is your catalyst to inspiring others to strive for excellence in themselves. You are the leader others follow. You feel great about yourself and you feel fulfilled knowing you are making your most positive impact through your influence. Those around you know creating their vision of becoming their greatest version of themselves helps achieve your vision. They know being connected with, and supported in, achieving your vision gives them permission to become their authentically greatest and achieve their vision.

Authentic leadership excellence is not something we achieve, check off the box, and move onto the next thing. Authentic leadership excellence is our lifetime journey of growth, impact, influence, and inspiration. We inspire others to become their greatest. They positively impact, model excellence for, and inspire others to become their greatest, and it continues.

Become the Great Leader our world needs!

# About the Author

Susan J. Ryan, MS, ILEC, NLP, ICF, guides individuals who are committed to unprecedented success in their business and lives, become their greatest, *and* become the leaders others follow. She is a best-selling author, international speaker, coach, and trainer. Sue founded her firm, Susan J. Ryan, to build great leaders from their inside out so they continuously achieve their most positive impact and collectively lead others to theirs.

As a dynamic communicator, Sue invites her audience into their potential and possibilities through storytelling that inspires, challenges, and awakens their unquenchable curiosity. Through coaching, clients raise their self-awareness of *who* they are and gain clarity about their uniquely greatest talents, skills, and abilities – their Prodigy Zone™. They connect with their purpose and create their authentic vision that evolves with them throughout their lives, continuously inspiring them and those they lead. They feel fulfilled and they great about themselves as they create their uniquely positive impact.

For more than thirty years, Sue has been modeling this with individuals, from solopreneurs to Fortune 100 C-Suite leaders, in more than 600 organizations, across a multitude of industries.

Sue's most recent book, *Our Journey of Love, 5 Steps to Navigate Your Caregiving Journey*, is a guide for caregivers that incorporates lessons from her more than thirty years in roles as both a professional and a caregiver. This intersection adds a powerful layer of insight to support individuals, in either or both roles –- and in all the aspects of their lives – as they lead themselves and others.

**Connect with Susan J. Ryan on Social Media:**

LinkedIn: https://www.linkedin.com/in/suearmstrongryan/

Twitter: https://twitter.com/CreativeBCoach

Instagram: https://www.instagram.com/creativebusinesscoaches/

Facebook: https://www.facebook.com/CreativeBusinessCoaches/

Email: sue@sueryan.solutions

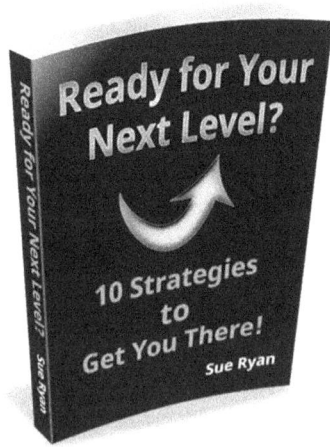

Download your free gift here:

https://info.creativebusinesscoaches.com/peak-performance

# How Business Culture Can Enhance (or Detract) From Your Client Base (and Profits!)

By Kyria McGill

After over 20 years in the human resource field, the one thing that I have learned (and embraced) is that people are important. While that may sound simple or common sense, a lot of business owners and leaders unknowingly allow other factors to take center stage – things like profit, research, growth, etc. Every aspect of business, from teams to clients, are created by, with, and for people – regardless of industry, demographics, or location. Culture is created by people – and a positive culture is the key to a business's success. The culture of an organization will establish a cadence for all other aspects from marketing to development, client satisfaction, and productivity. The question then becomes: How do you create a culture that resonates with your business vision, your team, and your customers? While the answer sounds simple – treat everyone positively – implementation is anything but simple.

Perhaps you are thinking "my business is a success already" or "my team is happy" or even "this is a business; people are here to work, not socialize." These may all be true – and that is great – but culture can make it even better; and by better I mean greater success, happier teams, and more profits (that is why we are in business, after all).

Here are a few facts highlighting just how important culture is:

- 82% of people believe that culture is a potential competitive advantage[17]

- Engagement and culture are listed among the top five global business strategies for executives around the world.[18]

- Highly engaged teams show 21% greater profitability.19

- The Engagement Institute states that disengaged employees cost U.S. companies up to $550 billion a year (yes, that is billion!).[20]

- Culture can determine success or failure during times of change: mergers, acquisitions, growth, and product cycles can either succeed or fail depending on the alignment of culture with the business's direction.[21]

Culture matters. Your business already has a culture, but is it the right culture? Is it an effective culture? Does your culture reflect your core values and expectations? Uphold your mission and

---

[17] Marc Kaplan, B. D. (2016). Shape Culture - Diversity Strategy. Deloitte.

[18] SHRM. (2017). Developing and Sustaining Employee Engagement Toolkit. Retrieved from SHRM: https://www.shrm.org/resourcesandtools/tools-and-samples/toolkits/pages/sustainingemployeeengagement.aspx

[19] Beheshti, N. (2019). 10 Timely Statistics About The Connection Between Employee Engagement and Wellness. Forbes.

[20] Beheshti, ibid

[21] Kaplan, ibid.

share your vision? As the world changes how and why we do business, the people we work with have changed, and our clients have changed. So, our culture continuously has to change, too.

But what is culture? For the purpose of business, we can define culture as: The character and personality of your organization – it is what makes your business unique and the sum of its values, traditions, beliefs, interactions, behaviors, and attitudes.[22]

I am the Founder and Culture Creator for CLM Business Solutions. Our goal, and my passion, is to help business owners identify the culture they have, determine the kind of culture that supports the mission and vision of the business, and then provide them with the tools to make it happen. Positive and profitable culture is not something you simply think about and hope for; it takes evaluation, strategy and planning, time, and, most importantly, buy in from the leadership and team. Culture is an ever-changing concept. Businesses need to have a strong foundation that is consistent and understood. Leaders need to evaluate the current team, review opportunities, and elicit feedback from the team and clients. All of these factors are key to planning, transitioning, and evaluating your culture.

So, that's a lot of official, technical, stuffy words to say simply that People Matter! A few years ago, I worked for a well-known organization, reputed to be a decent employer (decent, not awesome). I was an HR department of one, supporting a team that provided a difficult, physically and mentally, draining service.

---

[22] ERC. (2019, February 1). Workplace Culture: What It Is, Why It Matters, and How to Define It. Highland Heights, Ohio.

They provide support for families dealing with some of the worst life has to offer and yet they came to work each day, able to laugh, share, and support each other. They decorated their space, they smiled in the halls, they listened to their clients. They made a difference and their ability to be positive and bring some sort of joy was praised over and over by their clients.

Sounds like a pretty awesome group of people with whom to work doesn't it? And they were...at first. Change is always difficult, but changes in the workplace, small or big, can affect not only the internal dynamics, but customer interaction as well. Change creates uncertainty, resentment, fear, confusion, and even excitement and joy, all at the same time! That's a lot of feelings to wrangle on top of completing your actual work.

Now let's go back to the awesome group of employees, those happy, supportive people going out each day with a smile. Here comes the change. Enter in a new director – someone from the outside, new to the organization, with a track record of successes...basically the perfect person, right? This director was known as a result-driven leader (doesn't that sound warm and fuzzy?). What looks good on paper does not always translate to real life. While this director had the quantifiable skills, such as understanding our systems and spreadsheets, and so forth, is one thing; but there was no understanding of the culture, of what made the team cohesive, and certainly no ability to bring their best each day, for each client, and with each other.

At this point, it should be clear things changed quite a bit with the new director and, sadly, not all the changes were positive. The clients were still receiving service, the reports and paperwork were all in order, the I's dotted and the t's crossed – again it looked great on paper. Over time, turnover increased, customer satisfaction decreased, the vibe in the hallways was somber, support and collaboration decreased, smiles were rare, and laughter even more so. In other words, the culture had changed within the department and the effects rippled. Clients were less likely to provide positive feedback, less likely to reach out and share the positives. Basically, what had started out as a positive environment morphed into a somber, business focused, sterile place to be.

Now let's look at things from a different perspective – the goal is to create positive environments, after all. Early in my career, I had the privilege of working with a person who had such a unique (at least to me) approach to leadership (leadership – not management – but we will talk more about that later). While I am lucky to call her my friend many years later, the techniques I learned, observed, and later implemented shaped my personal leadership style and foundation for my business, team, and clients (yes, I include my clients as part of the culture). What I adopted was a technique for listening, of being present and engaged, asking and understanding the unique whys, and always looking for opportunities to help them strive for success (their idea of success can be almost anything – as long as it's important to them). It's a subtle process, requiring an authentic approach, and time to build. The journey is part of the process.

This team enjoyed being at work, there was very little turnover, customer satisfaction was high, and people simply enjoyed being in the environment (even if they weren't working) and displayed pride in what they did and loyalty to the team (not the job) of which they were part. This pride inspired ownership, which inspired confidence, which then increased sales!

These two organizations are not unique, they are not without good and bad, and both cultures take time and similar processes to achieve. What is the problem? The problem is clear that negative culture creates negative vibes, lower employee and client satisfaction, and smaller bottom lines.

The good news is the solution is simple – change the culture. (Wouldn't it be nice if that was all there was to it??) The bad news is that changing culture is difficult, time consuming, and constantly needs to be evaluated and updated. It is not a one-time fix.

While the concept of positive culture is simple and the solution is difficult, it is extremely important. Creating a positive culture and focusing on engagement will affect your profits. Yes, I said profits! We all want to make to make more money (isn't that why we go into business?). Creating a positive culture is a win/win/win (oh, and your competition is doing it!).

Now let's get into the practical part of things...how do you create a positive culture? Unfortunately, there is no fail-safe plan with step-by-step instructions, but here are five strategies that will help you start creating a culture that fits your business, supports your mission and vision, and increase your profits!

Step one is to plan. When you think of a great place to be, to spend time (and money), what are some of the factors that make the difference? What does that culture look like? Is it internally and externally the same? In a perfect world, what would that culture look like in your organization? This is the time to think big...over the top, crazy ideas (some of those become the best options), talk with your team, get input on what is working and what is not. Go old school and talk with your team, really listen to what they are saying, be open, make a list of pros and cons. Think back to when you started your business – you didn't just hang a sign and start selling. You created a plan, a budget, a design – it took time to find the perfect product, the logo, the team to help make it a success. Creating a culture is much the same – it takes time and planning, trial and error.

Step two is to share that plan with the team and get buy in. Your plan can be focused, inclusive, and exactly what you think it should be – which is great – but without the team's input and buy in you will not have accountability, ownership, pride, and, most importantly, support in creating a consistent culture. While many people like the idea of no rules, or freedom, teams thrive with a strong foundation and a clear understanding of what is expected. Teams that are all on the same page, understand the vision, support the process, and take pride in what they do, are accountable for their work, and have a sense of security for their job.

Step three is the tricky part. Evaluate your current culture. This evaluation is key to any kind of change and takes quite a bit of self-reflection. Good or bad culture stems from the leadership – which means we must look at our role within the culture first. Take a hard and realistic look. What are you doing to create a positive environment? Are you inclusive? Are you authentic?

Would your team answer these questions in the same way you are? Once you have an honest and thorough self-evaluation, let your team do the same. Be sure they understand that this is a safe process that needs to discuss the tough topics. Provide them an opportunity to evaluate the organization; evaluate their contribution and evaluate the systems, policies, and collaboration. For some businesses, this is easier done by an outside source because teams can be candid and provide honest feedback when it is anonymous.

So, now you have a vision, a strong foundation, and evaluation from yourself and teams. Lots of very valuable information – but what do you do with it all? For step four, let's go old school again. Take your original list of good and bad and compare it to the evaluation. Identify two or three areas that are clearly important to your team and your plan. Be realistic in the options. Are there any simple, cost-effective options that can be implemented with little or no effort, but high returns? Every item on the list will impact the culture. Create an action plan that highlights quick fixes, long term goals, and unattainable (for now) options.

In step four, the fun begins! Share the action plan with your team. Get feedback, build excitement, and get buy-in. Involve everyone in the process; more support makes for easier changes. As you are (presumably) looking to create a positive culture, go all out on this part. Make a splash, make it important, make it fun, start off the change by demonstrating the type of environment you are trying to create. Look to create a more relaxed environment that fosters free thinking and opportunity to take risks – ensure that your roll out reflects that – everything from the venue to the style of presentation sets the tone. Not sure what to do? There are great resources to help organizations create authentic and strategic events focused on the culture you are striving for.

So now you have your plan, your lists, your action plan, and the buy in from the team. Things are moving forward. People are focused and excited. So, how do you keep things going? Step five is...do it all again! Keep evaluating, keep asking for feedback, keep ensuring that items are being completed from the action plan. Celebrate your successes. Each time an action item is implemented (and successful), celebrate – no matter how big or small the item is. Celebrate. Stay positive. Highlight the opportunities. Did you implement an action item that didn't provide the outcome you had hoped for? Be honest and transparent. Don't place blame, but include the team in looking for alternative ways to accomplish the goal. Take risks when possible – status quo is neither inspiring nor beneficial to growth.

When you think of successful organizations that have created a strong culture, my guess is companies like Google, Disney, Nike, and so forth come to mind. We have all heard about the basketball nets in the hallways and the 24-hour buffet, or the flexible schedules and people riding bikes around or lounging on couches during brainstorming sessions. Are these all positive to the culture? That depends on your vision. Are ideas like this doable for all? How can you scale action items to it your vision and your team?

These five steps are just a big picture look at how to create a culture, and each step would be a book on its own. After over 20 years in human resources, this process is one of my favorite things to work through with business leaders. CLM Business Solutions works the desired culture of our clients into each project – from the employee handbook to engagement events. It is a never-ending process: The ability to take a vision and create the tools to make it happen – to see results through the eyes of the team, the pride, and (yes) the profits.  We all want a great place to work, with strong individuals with whom to work who are capable, knowledgeable, and able to look outside the box for new and innovative ideas. The challenge is creating the space to make those things possible.

"If you can visualize it, if you can dream it, there's a way to do it"
~Walt Disney

# About the Author

Kyria McGill has been working in Human Resources for over 20 years, bringing a strategic and business mindset to helping businesses create a culture that engages, educates, and empowers their teams. Kyria has a BS in Business Management, an MBA, and holds a SHRM-SCP certification. Having worked in a variety of industries from retail to janitorial, and a wide range of organizations from startups to Fortune 150 companies, Kyria combines experience, education, and a bit of fun to support companies' missions, visions, and core values. Kyria has been married to an amazing man for over 20 years, is raising 3 teenage boys, and as a family they enjoy movies, comic cons, and anything Disney!

You can download a free culture checklist by visiting Kyria's website at www.clmbusinesssolutions.com.

# 7 Easy Ways to Create Lasting Customer Relationships by Leveraging the Power of FB Messenger

By Meiko S. Patton

## The Problem:

As a business owner, you are constantly being bombarded with information coming from all directions. To say the least, this can be overwhelming and, frankly, exhausting. But you know you need to continuously connect with people and grow your customer base because that's how you generate more revenue.

## The Solution: Relationship Marketing.

This is very different from traditional marketing in which your entire focus is on increasing your traffic and getting leads ready for a sale.

In relationship marketing you must change your entire mindset. To be successful, you must focus on creating conversations that connect on an emotional level with your prospect. You have to learn how to earn your clients' trust first before you begin to sell to them.

One of the best ways to do this is by being vulnerable. Let your potential customer see your ups, downs, failures, and triumphs.

In relationships, you want to learn about a person's likes and dislikes, about the things that interest them, and the issues they find important. When you put the other person first in a relationship, your connection with that person deepens. And when executed genuinely with your potential customer, your sales could potentially skyrocket.

I interviewed Rachel Miller, owner of Moolah Marketing, and she told me that she lives by the rule of seven in her business. She interacts with her customers seven times before she ever asks them to buy from her. In fact, she said that often her community asks her when they can buy because they are so eager to learn more from her. Rachel is a giver and because she gives and develops a relationship with her prospects first, she has been able to generate multiple six figures in her business.

Nowadays, customers want to feel valued and they want to buy from people they know, like, and trust. Great relationship marketing caters to these needs without being sly, cunning, or manipulative. Genuine rapport happens naturally as you engage with your customers. And the icing on the cake is that if you value your customers and make them feel like they are being heard, they will become your biggest advocates. They will talk about your brand and word will spread about the amazing things you do and your sales will soar. This word-of-mouth marketing won't cost you a cent because you've taken the time to develop a relationship with your customers.

## The Opportunity

Facebook (FB) Messenger is a great way to establish relationships with your potential customers.

Question: Do you enjoy receiving messages from the people you like? Me, too. That's exactly what FB Messenger is. It sends text messages through the FB Messenger App from the brands you love and trust. And the cool thing is that you can opt out or unsubscribe anytime you wish. These messages are often called messenger bots or chatbots.

## What is a Messenger Bot?

Think of it as email marketing on steroids. Email "open" rates hover around 10 percent to 20 percent. FB Messenger bot open rates are currently at a staggering 80 percent to 90 percent. More people open these messages because they are always with their phones. That's why relationship and conversational marketing is here to stay.

Relationship marketing focuses on putting the customer first, thinking about the long-term relationship as opposed to a one-time sale. This form of marketing can help you create the know, like, and trust factor that ultimately leads to a loyal customer base. FB Messenger and chatbots are tailor-made to help make this happen effortlessly. Here are seven ways to do just that.

## 1. Offer a Free Lead Magnet

The best way to forge a stronger relationship with your potential customers is to offer them some valuable, free content. This is crucial at the initial stage of your client-getting relationship. You can easily do this via your FB Messenger bot and, from there, you can let the conversation flow.

An example of a lead magnet might be:

- An eBook
- A downloadable PDF
- A free video training
- An email series delivered through your bot
- A case study
- A discount coupon
- Your latest podcast episode

You can offer your free lead magnet through your website, social media, or my favorite, a simple QR Code, that, when scanned, opens a conversation in Messenger. Then your bot can send the initial message with the free piece of content. Relationship marketing is all about developing an emotional connection with your customers. Chatbots or bots are the easiest way to do that.

## 2. Ask Strategic Questions

Once you've hooked your customer with your free lead magnet, it's now time for your bot to ask a few strategic questions so you can continue to get to know your customer. These questions will, of course, vary depending on the industry you're in. I read a book once that says that whoever asks the questions wins. When you are in the position to ask questions, you get to learn more about your prospect and you are in a position to win their business.

Questions strengthen a relationship and you can ask as many questions as you like in FB Messenger. Once you understand your customer better, you'll know exactly what they want and then you'll be in a position to cater to them through your suite of products and services.

## 3. Thank Your Customers

The sweetest words to someone's ears, and in this case, eyes, is their own name. A great way to deepen your relationship with your potential customer is to thank them, by using their name in a unique way with your chatbot.

You can also use your chatbot to thank your customers for making a purchase. You can also send them a discount code for making a purchase. You can send them to your latest podcast or YouTube video via Messenger. The possibilities are endless. When you say thank you, people remember and they will have a stronger affinity for you and your business.

## 4. Survey Says...

I don't know about you, but I used to love *Family Feud* and the host would always say, "And the survey says." But I digress...

With relationship marketing, you want a long-term customer satisfaction and your bot can definitely provide that. Most surveys are super boring. But if you send a survey through your bot, it can improve the user's experience because it's conversational and fun. The information you receive from surveys is marketing gold. Once you receive their feedback, you're able to cater to their specific needs. Relationship marketing, like a real-life relationship, is give-and-take. You must be willing to ask and listen and then implement.

## 5. Consistency is the new Currency

In any relationship, if you stop talking to that person for a long period of time, the relationship dies down and that strong attachment is lost. To keep the fire alive in a relationship, consistency is a must. The same is true with your customers.

FB Messenger is a great way to stay in touch with your clients. You can send them regular messages so they don't forget about you or your brand. Sending a chatbot message at least once a week is a great way to stay top-of-mind. But, unlike with other social channels, be sure to send messages that are valuable and that move the relationship forward.

## 6. Go LIVE

In order to develop that know, like, and trust factor, people must be able to see you. One of the best ways to be seen is to do a FB Live. I had the privilege of interviewing Molly Mahoney, founder of The Prepared Performer and she recommends going live at least once per week. When people see you consistently every week, they get to know you and your relationship with them deepens. Molly made six figures from one live stream. She suggests finding a common problem that your audience has and then go live and discuss the solution with them. Genius, right? She answers their questions in real-time, she gives away prizes. It's super fun and interactive.

By leveraging the power of relationship marketing with FB Messenger you can begin to develop that know, like and trust factor, quickly and effortlessly. When your customers trust you, they will buy from you. They will remember and recommend your brand to others.

## A Modern-Day Example: A Public Speaker

Relationship Marketing w/ FB Messenger utilizing QR Code Messenger Technology

How can you leverage the power of FB Messenger if you are a public speaker like Kristin Thompson, founder, The Rise Event and Speak Serve Grow?

One common complaint from speakers is that they would love to connect with every attendee at the event, but often they are not able to do so. With the power of FB Messenger, that has now changed forever.

Say you are speaking and you want to connect with everyone in the audience. One thing you could do is to give them a free gift, such as a copy of your slides or a free lead magnet while you are still on stage.

Simply add a QR Code to your slides and then ask everyone in the audience to scan it. Once they scan it, they will be added to your FB Messenger list. You can now begin to develop a relationship with them and go through the six things we discussed earlier.

After you leave the stage and proceed to your booth, you can easily put a QR Code on the following things so that when the person scans it, they are immediately opted into your Messenger list:

- Business Cards
- Books
- Flyers
- Posters
- Brochures
- Table Tents
- Invoices
- Calendars
- Product Packaging
- T-shirts, hats, etc.

A great way to get people to come to your booth is to incentivize them with a free giveaway. You can have a large poster of your giveaway and printed on it can be your QR Code. When a visitor scans the code, they can be immediately opted in to win a free prize or gift from you.

Another really cool way is the use of Near-Field Communication (NFC) Cards. This type of communication allows two electronic devices to communicate with each other. **The one I recommend**

**is A1 Cards.** You can instantly transfer your contact information to your customer's phone with just one simple tap.

I interviewed my friend and Founder of Walletly.ai and A1 Club, Rupert Samuel and he said that marketers are flipping out over what they can do with these cards and how they can be easily integrated with FB Messenger to keep the conversation going long after an event is over.

This is an awesome way for speakers to connect with their audience with just a tap of a card. These can be ordered online and given away as business cards to your audience; and when they tap on the card, they can immediately be imported into your Messenger list, CRM, landing page, forms, etc. The possibilities are truly endless with this tech.

If you're still not convinced, check out these stats:

Why use FB Messenger w/ QR Codes:

- 1.3 billion people use Facebook Messenger every day[23]

- Open rate for Messages is 80 to 90 percent

- You can drive consumer behavior by sending them snippets inside Messenger about your latest: video, podcast, awards, news, etc.

- You can send them free gifts directly in Messenger to keep you top-of-mind

---

[23] https://www.facebook.com/business/news/insights/why-messaging-businesses-is-the-new-normal

- With email, people always use fake accounts, thereby missing your marketing message; but with FB Messenger you know exactly who they are

- If a customer has a question about a product or service, they can get instant customer service support. We all know that in business, whoever answers first, gets the sale.

- 83 percent of college students use instant messaging, such as FB Messenger. So, if that is your demographic, you need to be where they are.

- This is by far the fastest and easiest way to get someone onto your messenger list or email list.

**Want to learn how to create a QR Code?**

Scan this QR Code to learn how and also get FREE VIP BONUSES: (For iPhones, simply hold your camera over the QR Code. For Androids, please download the QR Code App and then scan the QR Code.)

# About the Author

In 2008, while employed by the U.S. Postal Service as a letter carrier in Los Angeles, Meiko S. Patton's life was served a devastating blow when her 59-year-old mom was diagnosed and later died from colon and liver cancer. After her mom's death, Meiko spiraled into a deep depression.

One day, while contemplating suicide, the thought of a postage stamp popped into her mind. That thought saved her life. That was nearly a decade ago.

Today, Meiko is an Amazon #1 Best-Selling Author of How a Postage Stamp Saved My Life – 21 Powerful Tips to Defeat Depression, Skyrocket Your Self-Confidence & Achieve Your Goals. You can find it on Amazon here: https://amzn.to/2EyHYTs

Meiko helps entrepreneurs skyrocket their self-confidence by educating them on how they can leverage the power of FB Messenger in their business.

Meiko recently hosted the wildly successful 1st Annual Messenger Marketing & Chatbot Virtual Summit. She interviewed over 20+ world-class Messenger marketing gurus who are killing it in the Messenger arena. The Virtual Summit was geared toward helping business owners understand the power of Messenger and how they can leverage it to land more business. Listen at your leisure on her podcast, The Meiko Show.

Meiko's work can be seen on Entrepreneur.com, Huffington Post, Lifehack, BlogHer, Govloop.com, Fedsmith.com, Careers in Government, and Postal Posts

Meiko loves to travel, run marathons, volunteer in her community, count her steps with Fitbit, and learn new languages.

And yes, Meiko, still works for the U.S. Postal Service at its Sacramento district office.

To learn more go to www.meikopatton.com.

# Brand Visibility Video Campaigning

By Jessica N Clark

When I first began my creative career pursuit, I felt lost in a sea of creatives who did similar work, offered similar services, and who, honestly, I felt were better than me. Finding a way to make my own brand stand out and move past the imposter syndrome was one of the greatest challenges of my own career. I soon realized that one of the most beneficial ways to humanize my brand was to create video and image content that put forth a call to action specific to the needs of potential clients. In 2011, I rebranded our business and reopened RedFred Productions as a full production company offering video and photography. Through the years, my focus shifted from events to an in-depth video strategist for businesses from concept to completion. Screens are all around us all day, every day. I am determined to help businesses get their brand across them.

The beauty of utilizing video in a brand marketing strategy is that you can create quality content for just about any type of brand and business. Video can adapt to the needs of the business and can be broken down and changed for more content creation options in the future. For a moment, I challenge you to browse your social media platforms, swipe through a day's worth of posts. How many videos did you swipe across? Now watch the first 20 seconds of a couple that may pique your interest. Did any of these videos trigger a response? Videos, compared to text and still images, produce around 1200% more shares and interactions.[24] That is because social media values the connections video produces through the networks. By 2020, it is estimated that online video will make up more than 82% of all consumer internet traffic, which is fifteen times higher than in 2017.[25]

Video isn't a new strategy by any means; however, what has changed is that videos are now being shared across every platform. YouTube, Vimeo, Instagram, Facebook, embedded videos, the list goes on, which means there are so many platforms to reach a greater audience. Video is a way to bring your brand to life, to captivate an audience with emotion, connection, and memory. Video does exactly what text is just unable to do, it takes brand marketing strategy to the next level. Video can create an immediate authentic response or interaction and those interactions are what drives up your content reach. According to a Hubspot content trend research piece, 54% of participants said that they want to see branded video content over emails and newsletters (46%), social images (41%), social videos - DIY home videos (34%), blog articles (18%), and, finally, content in PDF form to download (17%).[26] These findings are consistent across international trends as well.

---

[24] https://learn.g2.com/video-marketing-statistics

[25] https://www.clickz.com/future-of-video-marketing/236245/

[26] https://blog.hubspot.com/marketing/content-trends-global-preferences?_ga=2.233139166.1384468249.1580429044-1560092706.1580429044

As business owners, we are consistently trying to make headway into new markets, get our brand in front of a greater audience, and create money-generating leads. In a world advancing technology on a daily basis and an audience with shortened attention spans, we are up for a challenge to produce content that authentically keeps people and, more importantly, potential clients, interested in the services or products we offer. According to a HubSpot video content trend, it is noted that brands that use video content on their website landing page increase their conversion rate by 80% and boost user engagement by 22%; when included with a product call to action, consumers are about 64% more likely to purchase your system or product. These numbers are definitely hard to ignore. Branded video marketing will continue to push forward with greater opportunities to reach new consumers. There is no better time to invest in visual marketing for your brand.

The length of the videos may be different, depending on the goal. Having any video under three minutes is optimal; but, the shorter, the better. In addition to a brief description of brand video types, I have also included the optimal video length for best engagement practices.

## Ready for Launch or Crowdfunding:

For brands that are just starting out, they may want to create a launch campaign, introducing their brand and their story/ mission. Relatable content that humanizes your brand in today's consumer market will authentically connect and resonate with potential consumers. About 2 - 3 minutes in length is enough time for an audience to become engaged, hear from the founder, and learn about financial goals/product offerings.

## Driven by Testimonials

This video strategy is incredibly useful, especially for service-based businesses. What a better way to identify with your brand than with the people who value your brand the most! Utilizing testimonials can have lasting effects and can be cycled through with new content; you can embed them on your website and share them with all facets of social media platforms. Capturing testimonials on video has a greater impact than simply using text; it is an opportunity for your current clients to captivate your potential client. Testimonials are best to keep between 60-100 seconds in length, these tend to be informational for an audience who wishes to hear more about your program or product.

## Document Your Talk or Program

This is a great strategy to create more sales funnels whether you are documenting your talk to book more speaking opportunities or selling your program. Capturing a branded event for future workshops is also a great way to utilize this type of video. The video length is determined by your presentation needs.

## Call to Action: Lead Generating

Create a lead-generating video specific to your brand. These videos have a call to action in them. An example would be presenting an issue, identifying the issue, and documenting how your service/product would solve the issue. Lead-generating videos are best to keep between 45 seconds to 59 seconds, capture your audience, and keep them watching until the end.

## Branded How To

How-to videos are becoming increasingly popular among all types of brands. Many influencers/bloggers use this strategy as an unboxing or to document their recipes or creations. How-to videos are also effective in time-saving strategies for businesses. An example would be a realtor/mortgage office documenting the stage-by-stage workflow in buying a home (what to expect). Keeping your how-to or tutorial video between 1.5 to 2 minutes will keep your audience engaged; time lapse can be used to shorten the process to main direction points.

## Commercial Concept

Commercial concept videos are utilized most often on television and streaming services. These are used to push your brand in a memorable way whether you have a slogan, a pitch, or humor. These videos are great for a business ready to launch a campaign to push a story, idea, or concept for your brand. Commercial concept videos are best kept between 30 seconds and 59 seconds.

## Animation

Animations and GIFs are relatively new to business strategy. Prior to recent advancements in software programs, the cost of animation services was exuberant and too costly for small businesses. The costs have decreased and are now a great and fun strategy to use in branding. From animating a brand logo, to creating a looping animated shirt for the next boutique sale, the opportunities with animation are truly endless.

## Live Streams

Live streaming is a great way to authentically meet your clients across platforms. You can host Q & A, live sales, or information-als to an audience that can participate live. While it is easy to host live videos, it is still important to have a plan of action and keep your live on brand and on task. Having a clean space that aligns with the tone of your brand, as well as a quiet environment, will keep your audience engaged.

While the idea of diving into video and using it as a consistent marketing strategy is admittedly a little daunting to do alone, I have some great tips on getting started in effectively planning your own video campaign.

### 1. What is your market purpose or message you want to convey?

Simply wanting to sell more services or products is definitely an end goal; but, for the purpose of brand strategy, we want to have a specific goal forecast for your video marketing campaign. Identify your target audience and set a campaign goal: do you want more sales? Are you creating brand awareness? Website traffic? Knowing your audience helps you set the tone for your video campaign and it can be helpful to do some consumer stud-ies and research before jumping in.

## 2. Determine the type of video(s) you are planning to create

By determining which type of videos you plan to create, you can have a better understanding of costs, tone, and strategy to stay on brand throughout the video creation process. It can be confusing for consumers to see a variation of branding across your video marketing. Knowing your brand and staying consistent has a great impact on sale conversions. A study by McKinsey and Company shows that companies with consistent branding are 20% more successful than those without.

## 3. Determine a budget

Video costs can range in amount based on the project size, type, and whether you need actors, rented space, and/or equipment. You can expect to pay a professional $1,000+ for video services. Some companies (like mine) have a subscription option that can make video more obtainable on a smaller monthly subscription.

## 4. Make it a point to be inclusive

You may have noticed more captions in videos for social media, this is a great way to be inclusive to consumers and is soon going to be required for television broadcasts. It's also important to know that many consumers scrolling social media do so on silent so captions are still a way to captivate and inform your audience. Captions are also a great search engine optimization (SEO) tool for your brand. Transcripts and captions can increase page views, search rank, and increase engagement.

## 5. Decide who you will be working with to create your video content

## DIY it

We are increasingly becoming a "do it yourself" culture and while creating video can absolutely be done by yourself, be sure to set realistic goals because trying to learn new programs on the fly can be a really discouraging process. It is important that your videos have a standard of quality so if you do plan to create the videos among your own team members, it may be a good idea to take an online class to familiarize yourself with the programs you will use.

## Pay the Professionals

It is important to find and work with a company that understands your brand and the vibe of your mission. Find a few, schedule a consult, and work on a budget outline. Investing in a professional assures that you will have the tools to brainstorm your concept and someone to work alongside you to your campaign completion.

### 6.Upload across your platforms

YouTube is the highest trafficked video website worldwide and it's owned by Google, so your content can be linked across platforms and indexed for increased SEO rankings. Videos that are uploaded natively to Facebook have a reach 10 times greater than any other social media network. Your website landing page is a great place to add a video to as it has been shown to increase conversion rates. There are many other platforms to which can upload your content and you want to utilize as many as you are able to reach new customers.

Now your very first video has been produced and uploaded, you put it out into the universe, and now it will start rolling in the leads ... right? Well, in short, no; there is still some groundwork to do. This is where I work differently and how you can tell the difference between a video marketing strategist vs. simple video creators. Having a strategic plan to promote your videos is one of the most important steps in your campaign. In almost any business-specific platform you use, there are tools that generate engagement rates, view count, play rate, social sharing, and comments/interactions.

**Engagement rate** is a measurement of how many people have engaged with your post, if they watched, how long they watched, and if they skipped over your post entirely. This is a good indicator of how well you targeted your audience.

**View count** is a measurement of how many people saw your video in their feed and watched for the amount of time deemed by each platform as a "view." YouTube is 30 seconds, Facebook is 3 seconds.

**Play rate** is how many audience members clicked your video and watched natively; this can be affected by your thumbnail and length of the video

**Social sharing** and **comments** are simply the amount of interactions people have left with your video. A like, a reaction, or comment will drive up your reach by showing the platform that your content is interesting, which will reach more people. Sharing has a great impact on your video's reach.

As the wheels start to turn in planning your own video concepts for your brand visibility, it is important to remember consistency. Have you found your brand's soul? What is the feel or style of your branding? Do you have a motto or consistent tag line to add consistency across your videos? I would love to offer you a way to maximize your video campaign's financial return. Let's get you on your way to increase your brand visibility through a video campaign.

Visit www.redfredpro.com/contact to set up a free brainstorm consultation. We will work together to launch a series of which you are proud and one that represents your brand authentically to capture lead generating results.

RedFred Productions

www.redfredpro.com

@Redfredpro

References used in this chapter:

https://thegood.com/insights/video-marketing-strategy-statistics/
https://www.forbes.com/sites/mckinsey/2013/06/24/why-b-to-b-branding-matters-more-than-you-think/#29d73b0c59dd
https://www.criteo.com/insights/video-marketing-strategy/

# About the Author

Jessica N Clark

Jessica Clark is a visual brand specialist focusing on video and still photography for businesses. She began her photojournalism career as an events photographer until she met her partner through life, Brennan Clark. Brennan's background is film driven and naturally Jessica's focus shifted to working with businesses in creating authentic content through imagery and video.

As a child, Jessica was driven by creativity, she was often creating visual stories, through both imagination and storytelling. Her parents, as artists and performers, nurtured those gifts and throughout high school her artistic talents expanded to photography. Her path wavered from pursuing artistry and, like many, she set out on a focused, reliable, career path in nursing.

Photography continued as a hobby even as she leaned toward a stable career path, one that ensured her income and job security. However, she soon came to the realization that something was missing: passion. Her passion for photography overtook society's voice telling her had to follow a more suitable career path, and she did what she loved instead of the societal pressure for stability. Jessica has continued to do what she loves, and her passion makes the work she does all the more inspiring and important not only to herself, but to those around her. Opening a large brick-and-mortar studio space in Historic Downtown Gresham has given Jessica the platform and landmark space to become a leader in the photography and video industry. Her passion to create and navigate a male-dominated industry has opened doors for many other growing businesses, including aspiring photographers.

Jessica has earned herself international publications, Best photographer of 2018 by LOOKSLIKEFILM, along with several recognition awards such as Shoot and Share (2018 and 2019) and The Gresham Outlook's Best Photographer for 2020.

# Embodying Your Creativity to Success

By Lori Shin

## Can you hear the Call to Adventure?

What are you good at? What are you great at? What are you PASSIONATE ABOUT?

I really want to know.

If money were no object, and time plentiful, what would you do in the one-and-only life you have?

Up to now, you've been a master creator—perhaps consciously, or unconsciously. Are you open and willing to create your life by conscious design?

Since I'm good at guessing, I'm thinking that you've created your world from your life experiences, your environment, and your beliefs, habits, and actions. Am I close?

Whether you deem those very situations as good, bad, neutral, or horrific, as an adult you have been able to discern what has served you and what hasn't. What life lesson was highly useful, and what situation was decidedly toxic. And are you willing to shift what didn't serve you in order to open yourself to a new possibility? Will that trauma and drama continue sneakily and silently to hold you hostage? What if you can USE that drama and trauma to transcend that situation and heal, grow, and flourish in your creativity?

What gift or talent do you keep secret? Are you saying to yourself, "someday"? But, there isn't a weekday called "someday"...

How are you judging your own gifts, and your own life? Isn't it time to set yourself free, and unleash those gifts to the world?

All of us are on a creative journey of our own making, every single day. That includes me. It's that "Hero's Journey" that Joseph Campbell talked about. Maybe you don't consider yourself a "creative" person, but, I assure you, you are. Do you:

Listen to music?

Write social media posts?

Like to dance the night away?

Watch comedy or drama?

Daydream?

Take photos?

Take a bow (or curtsey, if you like). Yes, you are creative. How you are literally "embodying" your creativity (yes, I'm talking about using your body) can be one element on which you may be missing out; email me, and I'll provide some free guidance.

I want you to succeed, be seen and heard, get noticed. And I assist you by checking in – with your body – instead of checking out, looking for validations outside of yourself, and your innate knowing.

Why you? Because no one sees the world like you do, and your unique take on this planet may change not only your family and friends, but the creative, innovative abundant part you play in the theater of life may have impact that can change the planet.

You may think creativity is subjective. Well, yes, and no.

What you like, in, say, music, well, that's subjective.

But, scholarly researchers, such as Professor Mihaly Csikszent-mihalyi breathes light into what the Creative Personality is, as described in his book, *Creativity; Flow and the Psychology of Discovery and Invention.*

Feel free to email me for a free list of those personality traits, and some ways I give for you to foster creativity in your life.

Why do I feel creatives, entrepreneurs, and other individuals need to ignite all of their creativity, and set their world on fire with their unique gifts, right here, and right now? The planet needs your creative mojo. You are so very special; no one can do what you do. My mission and vision is to serve you in being a partner in your journey to be seen, heard, and inspire others with your gifts, and have some powerful, confident takeaways to use beyond our work together.

Will you answer the call to adventure, say yes to YOU, and allow the world to see you? What if you don't decide to heed the call? Will "someday" be too late?

I believe Marianne Williamson said it best.

*"Our Deepest Fear"*

*Our deepest fear is not that we are inadequate.*

*Our deepest fear is that we are powerful beyond measure. It is our light not our darkness that most frightens us.*

*We ask ourselves, who am I to be brilliant, gorgeous, talented and fabulous? Actually, who are you not to be?*

*You are a child of God.*

*Your playing small does not serve the world.*

*There's nothing enlightened about shrinking so that other people won't feel insecure around you.*

*We were born to make manifest the glory of God that is within us. It's not just in some of us; it's in everyone.*

*And as we let our own light shine we unconsciously give other people permission to do the same. As we are liberated from our own fear,*

*Our presence automatically liberates others."*

*—Marianne Williamson, A Return to Love*

# About the Author

Lori Shin is a creativity coach, and has been assisting creative and entrepreneurial individuals to embrace all aspects of who they are, by embodying their creative mojo, through online, one-on-one, and group coaching. Lori graduated from the Memphis College of Art (formerly known as The Academy), with a Bachelor of Fine Art, specializing in Graphic Design. She also dove deeply into the ecstatic dance world, tutored and mentored by Melissa Michaels, a leader in somatic education and dancework, based on the 5Rhythms practice of Gabrielle Roth, and continues to hold spiritual and embodiment dance events in the Portland, Oregon, area. She also incorporates games and improvisational skills in her group coaching in the Portland metro area. Lori also completed additional studies in Adult Learning, creating curricula for adults. She holds several certifications in life coaching through The Ford Institute for Transformational Training, with best-selling author, Debbie Ford. "I love emotional intelligence, improvisational work, and shadow work and I allow that work to come through in my creative workshops. I help you see how our individual and collective shadow can help or hinder living our life on purpose. Shadow work is the work of the brave warrior living within each and every human, and I am here to help you with understanding the shadow can unlock your unique brilliance." Email Lori at info@lorishin.com. Visit her at www.lorishin.com

# The Art of Authenticity in Business

By Mairin Moore-Cane

As the owner and principal Event Planner with Oak & Ivy Events and Design, our goal is to create authentic events that represent the clients' business, as well as meeting the desired effect of the event. I often encounter clients with blank faces in planning and strategy sessions. Their glazed-over expressions tell me they lack clarity; however, all too often they are also unable to succinctly describe their business. Without words that are genuine to them, I frequently see clients defining themselves by comparing themselves or their business to someone else or another company. Commonly, clients send me pictures from Pinterest representing what they hope to see duplicated and created for their event. The problem is that it doesn't represent who they are, or their brand; it's not authentic. Their selections may be related to popular trends or may catch their eye because of the splendor, but don't reflect their firm's branding or the message of what they are and stand for. It confuses them, as well as their audience and clientele; so, I work to help produce clarity for them in their events.

Together, we explore who they are and the purpose they have for their business. Unfortunately, I commonly see little energy and excitement in their eyes because they have forgotten who they are and their original mission in the operation. Their authenticity is missing, as is the joy and passion they had when they started their business. Sustained passion and stamina are imperative to be a successful entrepreneur. These are not possible if you are not fulfilling your <u>own</u> dreams, missions, and goals. Really, why does one start a business? At one point there is a passion to do something unique and distinctive. The loss of authenticity and individuality impacts the vigor with which one pursues the business and subsequently affects its success.

As successful entrepreneurs, we must be committed to our work because we dedicate a large portion of our lives to creating, building, and sustaining our business. We work long hours and make sacrifices. This amount of dedication is motivated by a passion for our mission, our dreams, and our goals. These are fundamental in determining how we approach our business and should be showcased in everything we do. They are the elements that drive us and must continue to motivate us in the difficult times.

Yes, there are times we work seemingly endless hours, and in stressful moments we may question ourselves and our purpose. This is why we must be driven by authentic motivation and passion, and our mission must be dear and held close to our hearts. Living authentically will be evidenced in our efforts and the energy we have to dedicate in which to work, to the quality of our work, and to the success of our business.

Often, I hear of and see individuals who get lost in all the effort it takes to make a business succeed and thrive; the chaos of trying to endure a competitive world in which the attention span of our audiences is mere minutes. They struggle to keep up with all that pulls them at today's distracting pace. Drowning in to-do lists, scraping to remain competitive, and searching for the path to success, the entrepreneur and his/her business loses authenticity and brand. The entrepreneur finds himself/herself duplicating another business in an effort to succeed. Your business must be specifically tailored to you, like a comfortable suit or outfit. It must fit all aspects of who you are. Rather than your being distracted and uncomfortable with wearing someone else's clothes, authenticity will allow you to be comfortable in what is tailored to you. You will be able to stand up confidently and boldly as yourself to represent your authentic business at its best.

The art of authenticity is remembering that who we are in business also reflects in the genuine relationships that are built with our clients, vendors, and the teams we lead. Embracing all of who we are and genuinely holding that specific space demonstrates a confidence, a certification of our qualifications. Sitting comfortably in the values on which we founded our business, we prove to others why they began a relationship with us initially, solidly extending our own brand.

As an example, look at the powerhouse brand of Oprah; flawed, yet comfortable enough in her own skin, she validates her authenticity by openly sharing her truths, strengths, and weaknesses. She notes, "I had no idea that being your authentic self could make me as rich as I've become." She has built her brand and is one of the most recognized faces around the world, with one of the richest empires in the 21st century, and one of the greatest philanthropists in American history. In all of her work, she remains authentically human as she embraces the entrepreneurial spirit that naturally directs her. Even with Oprah's battles with her weight, along with her life's story, she maintains empathy and an ability to connect with her audiences. All that she has embraced as her individual and personal brand, along with her ability to relate to others, continues to propel her to a level of success known to few. Never comparing herself to others in competitive industries, the *Oprah Show*, her publications, receiving nominations for Academy Awards, as well as generating her OWN television network, she has impacted the world through interviews with thousands of people, sharing her reality, and relating to others. By truly being herself consistently throughout the years, she has built an enviable empire.

Lady Gaga represents another piece of proof of hard-earned success gained by being truly authentic and by not forgetting all that personifies who she is. She has employed the strength and weakness of her mental health in her message to the world that it is okay not to be perfect and yet not get lost among the others. She has been able to stand out as an advocate beyond her music and acting career, making her a familiar name in households and countries around the world. By being comfortable with herself, accepting herself as an imperfect human being, and normalizing her own mental health, she is able comfortably to give herself the room to succeed in her own way. Known for her outrageous costumes in which she performs, you never know what to expect in her performances. But, by speaking her truth, she remains consistently and intentionally authentic. It is her natural, genuine personality and spirit that embraces social diversity that allows her to celebrate the legendary status and love of fans worldwide.

How do we recover and express who we are and express authenticity to stay connected in order to succeed, to be fulfilled as an entrepreneur, reaping the respect and success we deserve?

We must determine and express our own truths, core values, and what constitutes our genuine selves. By being honest in our beliefs, expressing our own true emotions and opinions, never compromising our own moral values to succeed, and searching where our heart leads us to truth, we discover more confidence and infectious energy. We become stronger, assuring security that allows our clients to trust us.

It is also worth mentioning that by adhering to our authentic roots, we are able to build a reliable foundation for our businesses. With all our reasons why we are who we are and do what we do, placing ourselves specifically in places we are in the world, we stay grounded and are able to maintain the healthy balance of morality, accountability, and responsibility to family and friends, as well as self-preservation amidst the stressors that come with being an entrepreneur. Examining our family systems, our backgrounds, the environments in which we live, and our beliefs help us understand exactly who we are, why we do what we do, and why we hold our core values. Understanding ourselves allows us to embrace authenticity solidly.

This leads to the next point of self-awareness. You must acknowledge your own story, the trials and tribulations, and the lessons learned from those moments in your life to understand the value of what brought you to this place. You will be able to understand the process and be able to evolve authentically. Developing your passions, inviting feedback to help you grow, and creating the ability to relate through self-awareness will help you stand out as a leader and mentor. Understanding your leadership position and embracing a team effort in your own market will give you credibility among your peers in your competitive business and industry.

Accepting our vulnerability, with authentic confidence from previous lessons learned, we open ourselves to the truth at all times. Continual growth and development to remain our best will give us the ability to adjust to the ever-changing world. Regardless of our stories and lessons learned, we will have those moments when we doubt ourselves; however, by understanding that creeping feeling of doubt and the foundations of who we are, our passions, and missions, we can neutralize the doubt faster for more solid results. By examining all that we feel (even the doubt) and our thought patterns, we learn to break the negative patterns so we may process and move forward with the courage to stand without fear and embrace all the opportunities and blessings we have been given.

With lifelong development, we find ourselves motivated to share. Inspiring others allows us to maintain balance by giving while reaping the benefits of being in touch with ourselves. This brings us full circle back to self-awareness and acknowledging who we are to sustain our own authenticity. Like physically working out, authenticity is like a muscle that must constantly be used to remain strong to ward off apathy and lethargy. By always helping others, we not only embody our best self, we use the muscle memory of who we are to stay balanced. By helping others, we help ourselves.

By remaining consciously aware and not forgetting the authenticity of who we are, and not allowing ourselves to be distracted by something other than genuine, we are less constrained, we are fairer in business, and we find ourselves more valued and respected. Remembering who we are, we are able to build stronger relationships, successes, and longevity in our business. We no longer have to compare ourselves or our business to someone or something else. We, and our businesses, are defined by our unique authenticity. Our methods, our marketing strategy, and our overall professional successes are derived by the elements that make us unique and authentic.

Events coordinated to the originality of the individuals and the brands of the businesses are exponentially more successful in meeting the anticipated effects. As one who plans events that maintain the authenticity of the brands and originality of the business or individuals, it is my observation that these individuals and organizations truly succeed.

# About the Author

Mairin Moore-Cane is intentionally passionate about creating and celebrating her clients' unique brand and deep-rooted distinctiveness for ultimate success. With over 20 year's experience, her award winning, international business, Oak & Ivy Events and Design, Inc. is the result of her fervent focus on authenticity, as seen within the details of her strategizing, planning, designing and marketing events and experiences.

Her energetic passion to celebrate life, and all that it offers, contributes to her voice as a speaker and mentor in her dedication for a positive influence.

In her spare time, Mairin also volunteers in her local community assisting as a planner for her city's events, as chair to the school PTA/Booster Board, and in multiple non-profit organizations.

# Rock your Business on Facebook!

By Sherri-Lee Woycik

## Why Facebook?

According to Mark Zuckerburg, as of August 2020, Facebook has over 3 billion people using it regularly, and it's steadily growing.

With that volume of people using the platform, it's an excellent opportunity for business owners to get more visibility and exposure for their business.

Facebook has the best marketing tools available to the entrepreneur, and best of all, you can market your business without having to spend a penny. In fact, many businesses aren't even ready for Facebook ads and would do better just leveraging all the amazing organic reach available to them.

But don't think it's as simple as constantly posting about you and your business, this is not a "build it and they will come" scenario.

There are four specific steps you want to leverage to maximize this platform, AND most importantly, you want to be consistent.

This is a marathon, not a sprint, and if you want to build a sustainable, thriving business for your (and your family's) future, this is something you will want to be doing for the foreseeable future.

Here's how:

## Know Your Prospects

Before you can sell anything to anyone, you need to know them almost better than they know themselves.

I mean, other people are selling or doing what you do, so what makes you stand out? It's not your experience or the fancy words you use; it is all about how you make your prospect FEEL when they are with you.

Do they feel cared for? Do you feel like you know them? Do they want to hear from you again? Do they know that you want to connect with them on a deeper level than just the sale?

The question is: How do you do this on a massive platform like Facebook?

It comes down to knowing who they are. Yes, demographics play a role here, but let's go deeper than that. Are they married, do they have kids, what kind of car do they drive, what kind of music do they love, what are their hobbies... AND why do they want to solve the problem that YOUR products or services solve?

Keep in mind that their reason for solving their problem is likely not the first reason they tell you. They will tell you the very simple, basic, socially acceptable reason... you as the entrepreneur need to dig deeper and find out their deeper reason. This is the one they don't tell everyone, and they certainly don't tell people that they don't feel safe with.

Now don't worry if you don't know these answers right away. This is a long-term exploration of your prospects' needs that will allow you to create relationships built on 'know, like and trust.'

The more you know, the more you can create: resources, content, Facebook lives, programs, courses, memberships, lead magnets, and more. EVERYTHING that will guide the growth of your business for years to come, comes from knowing your dream prospect!

## Magnetize Your Page

Don't wait to learn everything about your prospects... that won't happen overnight; it's a long-term journey. So, start with what you do know to make sure your page stands out on Facebook and attract your prospects to you like a magnet.

There are many parts of your Facebook page that you will need to keep checking regularly and keep updated... we don't have time and space here to go into them all, so let's just touch on the top 3 spots on your page and how to use them to attract your dream prospect.

1) **Your Page Name:** This is one of the main parts that travels with your posts and that people will start to recognise... and should help your prospects know what it is you do for them. So, look at the name of your page and ask yourself, if you were seeing it for the first time, would

you know what you do? Not sure? Ask your prospects for their feedback.

2) **Your Profile Image**: This is the circle image on your page; it travels with all your posts and needs to be something recognizable for your prospects. Should it be your logo? Likely not if your brand is not hugely recognizable... and remember, people want to interact with people on Facebook, so make this an image of you. Let people see you!

3) **Your Cover Image**: This should show your prospects what YOU DO FOR THEM! This is NOT your business card! Show yourself working with people, the results of your products or service, you speaking on stage, before and after images so that when people see it, they think: "I want THAT!" AND change it often, weekly in fact. Facebook loves when you change your cover image and will make sure your prospects see that change more than most posts. So, use that to get more visibility!

I've put together a free Magnetize your Page resource to guide you through the process. You can claim it here: http://bit.ly/pgmagnet

## Stand out in the Newsfeed with High Engaging Content

Now that you know your prospects on a deep level and your page is a magnet and attracting your dream clients to you, you have to make sure that they see your content and connect with you.

Because if they "Like" your page but don't ever see your content, they will forget that they ever liked your page in the first place.

Your content needs to keep you relevant with them, keep you 'top of mind' and help you grow your relationship with them.

I hear people all the time saying that Facebook's algorithm makes it so that no one sees their posts and that Facebook is trying to force page owners into ads... but that's simply not true. Facebook just wants you to use Facebook the way they want you to.

So, what does Facebook want from you? To create content that connects and gets engagement (likes, comments and shares). You see, Facebook wants people to stay on Facebook AND be engaged, because when people are engaged and having FUN on Facebook, they stay longer on Facebook and have a good feeling towards it and are more likely to choose to spend more time on Facebook in the future.

And what do people who are on Facebook want? To be entertained, educated, and informed. They want distraction from their lives and the things that are going on. They aren't on Facebook to be sold to, but you can sell to them when you build relationships first.

And what's the best way to get people to SEE, like, comment, and share your content?

Making more of your content about THEM than about YOU!

Ask them questions, learn about them, give them reason to know you and to respond to you. Don't just talk about you, your business, products, and services, give your prospect a REASON to interact with you.

Most people make posts that are one-way communications. They give great info, trainings or lessons, and then wonder why no one liked, commented or shared. The Facebook newsfeed is faster than the German autobahn (where there is no speed limit) with several million "likes" being clicked every minute. People are looking for content that doesn't just talk AT them - they want to be included.

And one of the best ways to make this happen is to ask them questions about themselves, easy, simple beginnings to conversations, just as you would with a new friend you are meeting for coffee. That's what this is... the start of the conversation.

But what to ask? And how?

I've put together 25 Questions to Explode Your Engagement Resource and you can grab it here: **http://bit.ly/2t2wrm6**

## Biz Boosting Strategies to Super Charge Your Results

Getting people to like your page and interact with your content is just the beginning and now you want to super charge your efforts with a strategic Facebook ads strategy.

Don't worry, Facebook ads are something anyone can learn how to do and once you have the relationship and solution part of your business down, Facebook ads will help you to reach more people for a very low investment.

You don't need to know how to run all ads, but you do need to know how to run the right type of ads at the right time for where your prospects are on their journey with you.

They are:

a) Page Likes Ads – To get people to KNOW you.

b) Boosted Posts – To get people to SEE your content.

c) Traffic Ads – To get people to your website or landing page.

d) Conversion Ads – To track the cost of getting people to buy or sign up for things.

e) Messenger Ads – To start deeper conversations with people who need to know you.

And at the core of all ads, what every ad has in common is the copy and the image of your ads. They need to speak to your prospects, they need to make people stop scrolling past your content in the newsfeed, so that they stop and pay attention to you and what you are offering.

Writing copy that gets your prospects to take action and using images that stop them from scrolling by is as important as targeting in your ads.

Get started with writing high converting Facebook ads and selecting scroll stopping images with the Ultimate Facebook Ads Template and Workbook here: **https://bit.ly/fbadswrkbk**

## What's Next for You?

These are the first steps for you to grow a thriving and sustainable business on Facebook. Of course, there is more for you to do to fully leverage this huge platform, but this will get you started.

Being an entrepreneur can be lonely sometimes, but you don't need to figure this out by yourself. Don't spend any more of your precious time and money winging it, throwing things against the wall, hoping something will stick. When Facebook is used strategically, you can attract real prospects to you and grow your business!

If you are ready to go deeper with me, join me in the Badass Facebook Marketing Club and let's start building your business together! https://bit.ly/slwbadass

# About the Author

Sherri-Lee Woycik is the founder of the Facebook Profit Formula and loves teaching entrepreneurs all over the world how to use Facebook to grow and engage their communities, develop relationships and make more money so they can have the businesses and lives of their dreams.

She is a single mom of 2 young adults and created her business in the aftermath of her marriage ending, not only to support herself and her kids but to empower women all over the world to take control of their businesses, financial situations, and lives.

# 9 Steps to Writing a Client-Attracting Book

By Suzanne Doyle-Ingram

I may be the only book publisher in the world who has the following motto: "It's not about the book sales."

There's a good reason for this. Like many lessons in business, I learned it the hard way.

About ten years ago, when the economy was crashing and my business (a marketing agency) was failing, I decided to write a book. I had heard about Amazon's new self-publishing opportunities, and I thought I would try to take advantage of it. I researched what was trending and decided to write a gluten-free recipe book. But, because I was so afraid it would fail, I wrote it under a fake name, so one would know that it was me. True story!)

However, when I applied what I knew about internet marketing, like using specific keywords that people were searching for, I was able to turn the book into a bestseller on Amazon.

It was absolutely amazing! I could not believe it.

I was so excited that I continued writing more and more books. I wrote a total of seven books that year. By the way, I had three young kids back then and had very little time to write these books. Typically, I would make dinner, clean up after dinner, put all my kids to bed, throw in a load of laundry, and then write from 10:00 pm to midnight. Then I'd do the same thing again the next day. And the day after that. And yes, I was exhausted! But I needed to make money to feed my kids. Plain and simple.

It turns out that that I made several thousands of dollars on Amazon selling these books that year. But there was a problem. The only way people could find the books was if they were on the bestseller list and it was so much work keeping them visible! It seemed like every day I was blogging and tweeting and posting about my books and begging people to buy them. It was actually kind of revolting now that I think about it.

After writing all those "trendy" books, I decided to write a book about something I was really passionate about–women entrepreneurs. I wanted to create a whole series of books for women entrepreneurs because it bothered me when I learned that women go out of business faster than men and women make less money than men. However, when I launched this book on Amazon, guess what happened? Absolutely nothing happened! No one even noticed. I sold hardly any copies and it did not become a bestseller.

I wondered where I had gone wrong...

A few months later, out of the blue, I got a phone call from a nonprofit organization. They said that they had received some funding to look into why women go out of business faster than men and why women make less money than men. I was thinking, *Are you kidding me??* I nearly jumped out of my chair! I said,

"Oh my goodness. I wrote a book about that!" The woman I was speaking to replied, "Yes, I know. That's why I'm calling you."

I was offered a contract to work with them for five months. I also received two other contracts that year to coach entrepreneurs. At the end of that year, I sat down with my accountant and she told me something shocking. Apparently, I had made more money that year from those three contracts than all book sales combined!

That's when the light bulb went off for me. That's when I realized that the money is not in the book sales, the money is in what you do after your book comes out. Your book can be the greatest marketing tool that you ever have. It can position you as an authority and an expert in your industry (even if you don't feel like an expert). The key is this: Don't try to sell books; use the book to sell YOU.

People started asking me to show them how to write and publish a book so I put together a course, and the rest is history. I've now taught over 800 people how to write a book.

I've developed a very simple system so that business owners, coaches, consultants, and entrepreneurs can easily write a book and use it to position themselves as an expert in their industry.

## Here are 9 simple steps to writing your book

### 1. Purpose

Take some time to think about what you want your book to do for you. Do you want to use it as a tool to get speaking engagements? Do you want to use it as a lead generation tool? Do you want to give it out to potential clients? Do you want to give a copy to every person you've ever worked with? Do you want to have it as a lead magnet on your website?

It's essential to think about what you want your book to do for you. When you think of your book as a tool, it helps you to remove any emotional attachment you may have. Every business has a website, business cards, a phone number and so on. Your book is just another one of these assets. I see people all the time who call their book their "baby", and who are so emotionally attached to the book that when the book launches, if Oprah Winfrey doesn't start knocking on their door they feel rejected and disappointed. Make sure you remove any emotional attachment to your book and just think of your book as a tool. Ask yourself what you want your book to do for you.

Next, think about WHY you're writing a book. What is your why? It's really important to know the reason why you want to write your book. When you know your why it makes it so much easier; it brings everything into focus and actually makes it simple to write your book. For some people, their why might be because they want to make their parents, their spouse or their children proud. For others, their why is because they want to share their big, beautiful mission with the world. Your why is uniquely yours; there are no wrong answers.

## 2. People

Who are you writing your book for and how will it help them? I hate to break it to you, but your book cannot be all about you. You have to think about the reader and ask yourself, "What's in it for the reader?" People have very limited time nowadays. Everybody is so busy; you have to realize that you're asking your reader to give you five or ten hours of their time to read your book. So it better be valuable. It's crucial that you give some thought to who you're writing your book for. When you can narrow down your target reader and write as if you're writing to one person, then everyone who reads your book tends to feel like you've written it just for them.

## 3. Plan

You must start with an outline. Not having an outline is the biggest mistake that people make. If you do not have a plan for your book, it will turn into a big mess.

Imagine that you decide tomorrow that you want to drive from California to New York. You could just get in the car and head East, but the truth is it would not be a very direct route and you're probably going to get lost along the way. It's the same concept with your book. You must have a plan so that you can build a strategy around it.

Writing an outline for your book is easy. Start with 7 to 10 main points that you want to cover in your book. Think about your reader. What are the 7 to 10 main points that you want your reader to know?

## 4. Expand

Under each one of your main points, expand your outline by writing seven to ten supporting points. Each one of these supporting points needs to 'support' what you're trying to say. (That's why they're called supporting points. Makes sense, right?) To illustrate the main point, the supporting points can be stories or examples or statistics or steps. Almost anything goes as long as you're supporting your main point.

### 5. Reflect

At this point, you still have not started writing. Look at your outline and ask yourself, "How will this help my reader?" What are some of the things that your ideal client says to you? Reflect on that and put those questions/concerns in your book.

## 6. Action

Once you're satisfied with your outline, now it's time to take action! Start writing your book based on your outline. A simple guide to follow would be to write approximately 250 words per bullet point in your outline.

When you have a solid outline and you write your book following your outline, it becomes very easy to write. My students tell me this all the time. They say, "Suzanne, I can't believe how easy it was to write my book!" It cracks me up every time. It's not rocket science, I promise you. But if you have a solid outline and you write your book based on your outline, it will just flow right out of you. If you are writing a book based on your area of expertise, everything you need is already inside of you. You are already prepared. So, don't get caught up "getting ready to get ready" and just trust that you can do this.

## 7. Commitment

You must make writing your book a priority. It does take some work, but the good news is that it eventually ends. The more committed you are, the faster it is. Your book could be done sooner than you think. If you write for at least 30 minutes, six days of the week and write at least 250 words a day, you could easily have your book done in one to two months.

## 8. Polish

Once the first draft is finished, self-edit it twice, and then send it to a professional editor.

## 9. Publish

There are so many options for publishing these days.

There are hybrid companies (like mine) where we charge an upfront fee to take care of the proofreading, cover design, typesetting, getting the book listed on Amazon, etc. and then we hand everything over to you and give you 100% of the royalties from Amazon.

Traditional publishers, on the other hand, take almost all your royalties and take a very long time to publish your book.

A third option is to self publish your book. You can open an account at Kindle Direct Publishing for free and upload your book. Once they approve it, it's automatically listed on Amazon.

Regardless of how you get your book out in the world, remember that it can be your greatest marketing tool, and a lot of the work comes after the book is out, not before. You can use your book to get booked on podcasts, get hires to speak at events, teach a workshop, develop an online course... the sky is the limit!

As you can see, it can be quite simple to write a book if you break it down into chunks. Don't get ahead of yourself and worry about marketing. Just write your book. Better yet, get a coach to help you from the beginning so that you'll ensure it's a solid, client-attracting book.

To get you started on the right foot, I've put together a free book writing training. You can watch it here: http://prominencepublishing.com/free

# About the Author

Suzanne Doyle-Ingram is the CEO of Prominence Publishing. She's a best-selling author and co-author of 17 books. She has helped over 800 business professionals write books and get published.

Suzanne coaches and trains individuals on how to write and publish a business book, and how to use that book as leverage to increase visibility, open doors for speaking engagements, increase revenue, attract new clients and much more.

Suzanne offers FREE Book Writing training on her website at http://prominencepublishing.com/free

You can visit Suzanne's website here: http://prominencepublishing.com

www.ingramcontent.com/pod-product-compliance
Lightning Source LLC
Chambersburg PA
CBHW060614200326
41521CB00007B/767